It Happened In
the Old South

Thirty-Two Remarkable Events
That Shaped History

James A. Crutchfield

gpp

Guilford, Connecticut

To the memory of my mother, Frankie Alfreda Whitworth Crutchfield (1905–1992), a true granddaughter of the Old South.

Project editor: David Legere
Layout: Sue Murray
Map: M. A. Dubé © Morris Book Publishing, LLC

Library of Congress Cataloging-in-Publication Data is available on file.
ISBN 978-0-7627-4821-1

Printed in the United States of America

10 9 8 7 6 5 4 3 2 1

CONTENTS

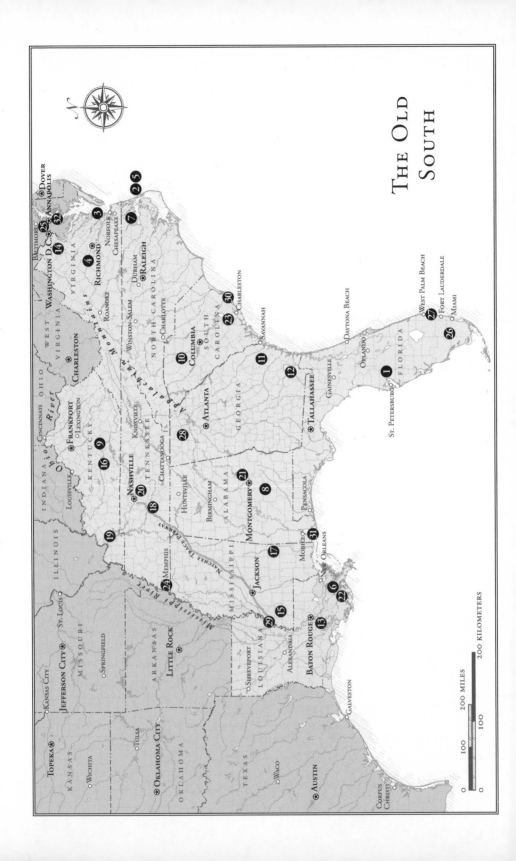

THE OLD
SOUTH

LEGEND

CONTENTS

PREFACE

This book highlights some fascinating episodes that have occurred in the long history of the Old South, that region of the United States that encompasses Virginia, North and South Carolina, Georgia, Florida, Alabama, Mississippi, Louisiana, Tennessee, and Kentucky. The time period is from the first explorations by Europeans in the sixteenth century to the end of the Civil War. A couple of District of Columbia events are included as well since, before the war, the nation's capital was more Southern in its culture, traditions, and lifestyles than it was Northern.

I hope that *It Happened in the Old South* will provide a few hours of pleasure to those who read it, and that it will perhaps find its way into the classrooms of the region, thereby giving younger generations a better appreciation of their vast heritage.

FLORIDA'S FIRST WHITE CITIZEN

Florida, 1528

Seventeen-year-old Juan Ortiz could not believe what was happening to him. Less than an hour earlier, he had been on board ship, moored in present-day Tampa Bay, chatting with his compatriots about the great adventure that they were sharing here in the New World. Now, after he had volunteered to go ashore to investigate what appeared to be a white piece of paper stuck in a tree branch protruding from the beach, he was literally running for his life. In pursuit were a score or more of yelling, tattooed Indian braves who were making no mistake about their intentions. As Juan looked seaward, he was horrified to see his ship and its crew heading out of the bay rather than toward the beach to give him aid. In less than ten minutes, the galleon had disappeared around a point in the bay and Juan was being manhandled by the Indians.

Ortiz was carried inland by his captors and later that day reached an Indian village, where he was placed in a hut and left alone to ponder his fate. Thoughts of the day raced through his brain, and he quickly reviewed the events that had brought him to this subtropical wilderness.

Although Christopher Columbus had first stepped upon New World territory nearly forty years earlier, excitement still ran rampant in Spain, where a constant stream of conversation flowed about the riches and glory to be found in the Americas. Young Ortiz was not exempt from all the chatter, and in early 1527 he volunteered his services to an explorer named Pánfilo de Narváez, a veteran of Columbus's second voyage to the New World. With five ships, the expedition left Spain in June of that year and arrived on the west coast of Florida on April 9, 1528, following a couple of stops in the West Indies.

Upon his arrival near Tampa Bay, Narváez divided his command into two groups—one, led by himself, exploring the mainland on foot; the other, consisting of the ships, coasting and observing along the western shore. Young Ortiz had stayed with the ships, and the piece of paper visible on the beach was thought by the crew's captains to be a message from their commander, hence the necessity to retrieve it. As it turned out, the supposed message was a hoax planted by the Indians to lure the Spaniards ashore.

By the time Ortiz had finished reviewing the events that led to his predicament, morning had dawned. Following a skimpy breakfast, he was led to the center of the village, where he was prepared by the natives to burn at the stake. As the flames rose around him, a young Indian maiden appeared out of the crowd and begged the warriors to release the Spaniard, then leaped forward and cut the bindings from his hands and feet. Ortiz fainted from pain and woke up in the maiden's hut. She was Acuera, daughter of a powerful chief of the Timucuan tribe and ruler of Ortiz's tormentors.

The Timucuan consisted of a consortium of many smaller tribes that at the time numbered as many as thirteen thousand members, spread across central and northern Florida from the Atlantic Ocean to the Gulf of Mexico. They were a powerful people who, as events turned out, would be abused by the Spanish explorers, including

Narváez himself. In 1910, Frederick Webb Hodge, a leading American ethnologist whose authority is still respected today, described the tribe as "tall and well made."

> *They went almost entirely naked except for the breech-cloth, but covered their bodies with an elaborate tattooing. They were agricultural, though apparently not to the same extent as the Muskhogean tribes, depending more on game, fish, oysters, wild fruits, and bread from the nourishing coonti root. Their larger towns were compactly built and stockaded, their houses being circular structures of poles thatched with palmetto leaves, with a large "townhouse" for tribal gatherings in the center of the public square.*

Hodge also reported that the tribe practiced scalping, mutilation of the dead, and religious cannibalism.

For three years Ortiz endured the hatred of everyone except Acuera; however, even her pleadings failed to gain him the acceptance of her tribesmen. Eventually, with the assistance of Acuera, Ortiz escaped the village and traveled overland to a neighboring town, where a kindly chief and his wife adopted the weary Spaniard into the tribe. For the next eight years, among the friendly and supportive natives, Ortiz became more Indian than Spaniard, until one day in June 1539.

Hernando de Soto had just landed in Tampa Bay, commanding the largest Spanish expedition to the New World to date—around seven hundred men, including a carpenter, a shoemaker, several tailors, a farrier, a sword maker, a few notaries, two engineers, and twelve priests, as well as two hundred horses, several hundred pigs, and a pack of ill-tempered dogs, all aboard nine ships. Upon landfall, de Soto dispatched a few horsemen inland to reconnoiter the region. They chanced upon Ortiz and some of his Indian compatriots and, after Ortiz identified himself as a Christian brother, the conquistadors took him back for an interview with their commander.

Although Ortiz no doubt had dreams of returning to his family and friends in Spain after all those years, it was not to be. De Soto recruited the Spaniard turned Indian, now turned Spaniard again, to be his official interpreter for the long expedition, which wound up occupying the next four years—the last nineteen months without Ortiz and the last sixteen months without de Soto, both of whom died in the Mississippi River valley. The journey eventually traversed parts of present-day Florida, Georgia, South Carolina, North Carolina, Tennessee, Alabama, Mississippi, Arkansas, Louisiana, and possibly Texas, covering several thousand miles during the effort.

After he died, Ortiz was sorely missed by the men of the de Soto expedition. One of the party's chroniclers wrote, "Throughout the entire exploration [Ortiz] had served no less with his forces and strength than with his tongue, for he was an excellent soldier and of much help on all occasions." Another declared that his death was "a loss to the Governor [De Soto] greatly regretted; for without an interpreter, not knowing whither he was traveling, Soto feared to enter the country, lest he might get lost."

The names of the great Spanish conquistadors have spanned the centuries—Hernando de Soto, Francisco Pizarro, Francisco Vásquez de Coronado, Juan Rodriguez Cabrillo, Ponce de Leon, and Cabezo de Vaca—most of them being easily recognized by students of American history. Yet, sadly, Florida's first white citizen, Juan Ortiz—the man who, through his language skills and intimate knowledge of the Indians, was largely responsible for any successes that could be claimed for the de Soto expedition—is largely forgotten.

LOOKING FOR THE LOST COLONY

North Carolina, 1590

As soon as Christopher Columbus stumbled upon the New World in 1492, the Crowns of England, Spain, Portugal, Holland, and France jumped into the arena and sent ships far across the Atlantic to exploit the newfound lands and garner what treasures they could. Consequently, during the 1500s, much of the New World was frequented by ships flying many different flags.

Spain, undoubtedly the world's strongest seafaring nation at the time, explored, and in many cases established strongholds in, the West Indies, Mexico, and the present-day Southeastern United States. In fact, in 1561 Pedro Menendez de Aviles accidentally came upon the Chesapeake Bay, spent a few days in what is now Virginia, and took Opechancanough, an older brother of the more famous Powhatan, back to Spain with him. Nine years later, when the Indian was returned to his own people, the Spanish churchmen who accompanied him established a short-lived Jesuit mission on the south bank of the York River.

By 1565, in the name of Spain's monarch, Philip II, de Aviles had established Saint Augustine in Florida, the oldest surviving

European-settled town in the United States. In the meantime Frenchmen were making inroads into today's Canada, while their English counterparts concentrated on the mythical land that soon became known as Virginia.

Queen Elizabeth I sat on England's throne at the time, and in 1584 she issued to one of her court favorites, Walter Raleigh, a royal grant that gave him possession of a large tract of land in America. Raleigh wasted no time sending out a party under the command of Philip Amadas and Arthur Barlowe to explore his new possessions. Landing in the vicinity of the Outer Banks of North Carolina, the Englishmen reported favorably to Raleigh upon their return home. Hoping to impress his virgin queen, Raleigh named the recently visited territory Virginia.

During the summer of 1585, Raleigh dispatched a colonizing party of some 107 prospective settlers to Virginia, under the guidance of Governor Ralph Lane. The ships disembarked on Roanoke Island, and over the next few months, the entire region along present-day North Carolina's Atlantic coast was explored. The winter proved difficult, however, and during the following summer, when Francis Drake's small fleet called on the colonists, the disheartened survivors jumped at the opportunity to leave the miserable place for England.

The following year (1587) Raleigh tried again to colonize his holdings. The new governor, John White, and about one hundred settlers returned to the area. On August 18 the governor's daughter gave birth to a girl who was christened Virginia "because she was the first Christian born in Virginia," wrote the proud grandfather.

After White assured himself that all was well, he set off for England to resupply. By the time he returned to Roanoke Island, three years had passed, the departure from his homeland having been delayed due to England's and Spain's flirtation with war and the invasion threat by the Spanish Armada. Yet he was confident on August 15, 1590, that all was well with the colonists he had left behind, later recalling that "we saw a great column of smoke rising from Roanoke Island, near the spot where I had left our colony in the year 1587." Continuing, he wrote that "the smoke gave us good hope that some of the colony were still there, awaiting my return from England."

On August 17, despite a horrific gale in which seven companions were lost in the sea, the party finally reached the shores of Roanoke Island. White picks up the gripping story:

> Before we could reach the place where the planters had been left, it was so dark that we missed it by a quarter of a mile. At the north end of the island we espied the light of a great fire through the woods. We rowed towards it, and when we were opposite the place we let fall our grappling anchor near the shore, sounded a trumpet call, and then played the tunes of many familiar English songs. We hailed the shore with friendly greetings, but got no answer. At daybreak we landed, and when we approached the fire we found the grass and some rotten trees burning. From there we went through the woods . . . [and] proceeded to walk along the shore, rounding the north point of the island, until we came to the place where I had left our colony. . . . During the walk we saw in the sand the prints of the feet of two or three savages which must have been made during the night. As we went inshore up the sandy bank we saw a tree on the brow of the cliff curiously carved with the clear Roman letters C R O.

White's hopes were raised somewhat since he and the colonists he had left behind had agreed upon a system whereby the returning governor would know if they had changed locations. According to the governor, they were to "write or carve on trees or doorposts the name of the place where they had settled, for at the time when I departed for England in 1587 the men were ready to move from Roanoke fifty miles up into the mainland." After combing the area for such signs, the men found none and moved on to the site of the previous settlement, but soon discovered that all of the dwellings had fallen into disrepair and that a stockade had been built around the building site. On one of the stockade posts were the carved letters CROATOAN. Further investigation unearthed no signs of life other than some cannon shot, iron bars, and a few fowling guns. Nearby, the men discovered a number of chests, three of which belonged to Governor White, that had been buried but later opened, supposedly by natives, and the contents spoiled.

Attempts during the following days to navigate to Croatoan, situated near present-day Cape Hatteras, proved impossible. On one of the ships, three of the anchors and anchor cables were lost, leaving only one set operational; the freshwater cask disappeared; and the food supply was nearly exhausted. The other ship was deemed practically unseaworthy. Plans were then laid for the flagship carrying White to sail to the West Indies for refitting, then return as soon as possible to continue the search for the lost colony. The other ship was ordered to somehow sail back to England.

Alas, it was not to be. Continued bad weather forced White to return to England, apparently now convinced that his countrymen, including his daughter and granddaughter, were truly lost forever.

White was next heard from in February 1593, when he wrote a letter from his home in Ireland to his friend Richard Hakluyt. With the letter was a detailed report of his failed mission to rescue the remnants of the lost colony. After this, White fell from the pages of history, not to be heard from again.

THE FOUNDING OF JAMESTOWN

Virginia, 1607

In 1606 King James I presented a charter to a group of English entrepreneurs to organize the Virginia Company of London, with authority to exploit, colonize, and administer the vast region known as Virginia. In December of that year, three galleons—the *Susan Constant, Discovery,* and *Godspeed*—slipped their moorings near London and drifted down the Thames River, soon to be surrounded by the mighty Atlantic Ocean. During late April 1607, after an eighteen-week-long voyage, the small fleet, commanded by Captain Christopher Newport, sighted Cape Henry at the mouth of the Chesapeake Bay.

Captain John Smith, who was one of seven counselors named to govern the colony, described the site of the first landfall in his book *A Map of Virginia,* published in 1612. "There is but one entrance by sea into this country," he wrote, "and that is at the mouth of a very goodly Bay the width whereof is near 18 or 20 miles." Continuing, he reported:

> *The cape on the Southside is called Cape Henry in*
> *honor of our most noble Prince. The show of the land*

there is a white hilly sand like unto the Downes, and
along the shores great plenty of pines and firs. . . .
Within is a country that may have the prerogative
over the most pleasant places of Europe, Asia, Africa,
or America, for large and pleasant navigable rivers,
heaven & earth never agreed better to frame a place
for man's habitation being of our constitutions, were
it fully manured and inhabited by industrious people.
Here are mountains, hills, plains, valleys, rivers, and
brooks, all running most pleasantly into a fair bay . . .
with fruitful and delightful land.

For two weeks following the first sighting of Cape Henry, New-port and his adventurers explored the numerous streams, inlets, and marshes along the Atlantic coast. Proceeding up one of the waterways—a broad river that dumped its waters into the Chesa-peake Bay and later was named the James in honor of the king—the three ships, crew, and passengers eventually moored near a spit of favorable-looking land situated near the north bank. The date was May 13, 1607, and the site selected for settlement was present-day Jamestown Island.

The roster of 105 new arrivals included four carpenters, two bricklayers, one blacksmith, one mason, one tailor, one preacher, one drummer, one barber, one "sailer," and two surgeons. Twelve others were listed as laborers, and the rest were classified as either members of the council, gentlemen, or boys. The amount of work that awaited so few skilled craftsmen was overwhelming, but according to John Smith, everyone pitched in. "The Council contrived [designed] the fort," he wrote, and "the rest cut down trees to make place to pitch their tents; some provide clapboard . . . some make gardens, some nets, etc." Smith also revealed that "overwhelming jealousies" among the new colony's leadership prohibited the formation of an army for defense or the construction of a fort, other than a poorly conceived one hastily built from "boughs of trees cast together in the form of a half moon."

Settling the new colony would not be easy for the Jamestown adventurers. Not only was the site ill-suited for European habitation due to intense humidity, hoards of biting insects, and poorly drained terrain, but also food supplies were either quickly depleted or ruined due to spoilage from the fierce heat. Four months into the audacious colonization scheme, fifty of the newcomers had died from starvation and/or disease. "Within ten days [of the original landfall on James-town Island], scarce ten amongst us could either go, or well stand, such extreme weakness and sickness oppressed us," wrote a dejected Smith several years later. But this was only the beginning.

Scores of pairs of curious eyes peered at the Englishmen as they went about their chores. The region was controlled by the Algonquian-speaking Powhatan, whose population of around nine thousand was organized into thirty distinct subtribes and scattered throughout more than a hundred towns and villages in present-day tidewater Virginia. The supreme authority of this loosely controlled confederation was a chief named Wahunsonacock, or, as the new arrivals would call him, Powhatan.

John Smith left a detailed account of the tribe, which included an essay on the lifestyles and living arrangements of its people, as well as a vivid firsthand description of the great chief Powhatan and his entourage:

> *He is . . . a tall well proportioned man, with a sour*
> *look, his head somewhat gray, his beard so thin that it*
> *seems none at all, his age near 60; of a very able and*

hardy body to endure any labour. About his person ordinarily attends a guard of 40 or 50 of the tallest men his country affords. Every night upon the 4 quarters of his house are 4 sentinels each standing a flight shoot from the other, and at every half hour one from the corps du guard doth hollow, unto whom every sentinel doth answer round from his stand; if any fail, they presently send forth an officer that beats him extremely.

Smith estimated that about five thousand natives lived within sixty miles of Jamestown, but guessed that only about fifteen hundred qualified as warriors "fit for their wars." This was, no doubt, sobering news, and the colonists must have been relieved when initial visitations by the natives turned out to be friendly. The relationship between the two peoples would not always remain peaceful, however, as the weeks, months, and years ahead sadly proved for both parties.

Although the first few years of the colony's existence tried the patience and wits of everyone there, it did survive, although sometimes, it seemed, by divine intervention. During the winter of 1609–10, the town was practically devastated by a combination of natural forces, including extremely frigid weather, an onslaught of uncontrollable communicable disease, and starvation. This horrible period has become known as the "starving time" and, before the spring days of 1610 brought respite, an estimated 90 percent of the town's inhabitants had died from one cause or another. Makeshift funerals for the recently deceased were daily occurrences. A contributor to Captain John Smith's book *The Generall Historie of Virginia, New-England, and the Summer Isles,* published in London in 1624, described the unbelievable conditions:

*Though there be fish in the sea, fowl in the air, and
beasts in the woods, their bounds are so large, they
so wild, and we so weak and ignorant, we cannot
much trouble them. . . . As for our hogs, hens, goats,
sheep, horse, or what lived, our commanders, officers
and savages daily consumed them, some small proportions sometimes we tasted, till all was devoured; then
swords, arms, pieces, or any thing, we traded with the
savages . . . that what by their cruelty, our governor's
indiscretion, and the loss of our ships, of five hundred
within six months . . . there remained not past sixty
men, women and children, most miserable and poor
creatures; and those were preserved for the most part, by
roots, herbs, acorns, walnuts, berries, now and then a
little fish . . . yea, even the very skins of our horses.*

Disease and famine were not the only factors that combined
to make the winter of 1609–10 one of starvation and near-disaster
for Jamestown's residents. Relations with the neighboring Indians,
under the leadership of Powhatan, were once again strained and, in
addition to bloody skirmishes between the two parties, the tribesmen
abruptly curtailed trading with the Englishmen for much-needed
food, thereby making survival a real issue.

Food was not a problem for the Indians, however. Agricultural
in nature, they grew everything they needed, or else they fished and
hunted the neighboring streams and woods. Now, however, partially
due to an imprudent trading policy that had been implemented
by Jamestown leaders—one that foolishly allowed weapons to be
swapped with the natives for food and other supplies—the Indians

were better armed than their adversaries and in a position to levy an attack at their leisure, should they desire. With these dark clouds rapidly gathering above them, Jamestown residents scurried outside the fort's palisades, scavenging any food they could, while the Indian foe watched and patiently waited.

Yet, despite years of trials and tribulations, Jamestown somehow survived and served as the Virginia colony's capital until 1699, when the seat of government was moved to Middle Plantation, or Williamsburg.

A TRIP TO THE
BLUE RIDGE MOUNTAINS

Virginia, 1670

Few people today can name the first European to behold the majesty and beauty of the Southern Appalachians, viewing the haze-covered peaks of the Blue Ridge Mountains from a spot just northeast of present-day Charlottesville, Virginia, on March 14, 1670.

John Lederer, a twenty-six-year-old German physician who had only recently arrived in the New World from Hamburg, was commissioned by Virginia's royal governor, William Berkeley, to explore the wilderness beyond the fall line, which represented the colony's far western frontier. Since many people thought that the streams issuing from the western side of the mountains flowed directly into the Pacific Ocean, Lederer construed his duties to include the search for the fabled Northwest Passage to Asia.

On March 9, 1670, Lederer, accompanied by three Indians, left the town of Chickahominy, situated on the north bank of the Pamunkey River, possibly in present-day King William County. The following day, in order to avoid the swampy ground between the Pamunkey and Mattaponi Rivers, his party crossed to the opposite side of the Pamunkey near the confluence of the South and North Anna Rivers. Today, Interstate 95 crosses this area some twenty-five miles north of Richmond.

By March 13 Lederer had reached the headwaters of the South Anna River, several miles northeast of Charlottesville. The following day, he climbed a neighboring peak and cast his eyes on the Blue Ridge Mountains for the first time. The moment was captured in a book published in 1672 in London, titled *The Discoveries of John Lederer in Three Several Marches from Virginia, to the West of Carolina:*

> *The fourteenth of March, from the top of an eminent hill, I first descried the Apalataean [sic] Mountains, bearing due West to the place I stood upon: their distance from me was so great, that I could hardly discern whether they were Mountains or Clouds, until my fellow Indian travelers prostrating themselves in Adoration, howled out after a barbarous manner, Okeepoeze, i.e.; God is nigh.*

It had taken Lederer's small party four days to travel the sixty miles across the relatively flat land from Chickahominy to this point. It would take four more days to cover the thirty additional miles to the crest of the mountains, somewhere near present-day Big Meadows. In the interim, Lederer reported seeing an abundance of deer, black bears, small "leopards" (presumably bobcats), wolves, beavers, otters, and gray foxes.

Finally, on March 17, the group reached the real mountains and Lederer wrote, "The Air here is very thick and chill; and the waters issuing from the Mountainsides, of a Blue colour, and Alu-mish taste." On the following day an excited Lederer scrambled up a nearby mountain to what he must have thought to be the top of the world. "After I had in vain assayed to ride up," he exclaimed, "I alighted, and left my horse with one of the Indians, whilst with the other two I climbed up the Rocks, which were so incumbred with bushes and brambles, that the ascent proved very difficult." But the undergrowth was not the only hindrance with which the explorer had to contend. Continuing, he added that "besides, the first preci-pice was so steep, that if I lookt down, I was immediately taken with a swimming of my head."

Either Lederer was a romantic or he was trying to impress the readership of his future book when he erroneously claimed to have seen the ocean from his perch high in the Blue Ridge. He wrote,

> *The height of this Mountain was very extraordinary: for notwithstanding I set out with the appearance of light, it was late in the evening before I gained the top, from whence the next morning I had a beautiful prospect of the Atlantick-Ocean washing the Virginian-shore; but to the North and West, my sight was suddenly bounded by Mountains higher than that I stood upon.*

Over the next few days, Lederer searched frantically for a pass in the mountains that would lead him farther westward, but the com-bined cold weather and deep snow severely restricted his movement. Grudgingly, he descended from the highlands and, with his three Indian companions, "returned back by the same way that I went."

On May 20, 1670, not satisfied with his initial feat, Lederer left the settlements a second time in another attempt to get beyond the first chain of the towering Blue Ridge. This time he was accompanied by twenty mounted settlers and five neighboring Indians. His point of departure was the Falls of the James River, near present-day Richmond. Striking out due west, the party traveled overland to the James River near its confluence with the Buffalo River. Turning south, Lederer led his group toward today's North Carolina state line. However, before much progress was made, most of his companions decided to return home, leaving the German explorer with only one Indian with whom to continue the journey.

Near where the John H. Kerr Reservoir is now located, the two wanderers crossed into North Carolina. Making a wide southwestward sweep, they progressively explored the headwaters of the Tar, Neuse, Cape Fear, and Pee Dee Rivers before reaching the farthest point of their journey near Rock Hill, South Carolina. Another turn eastward brought them past today's city of Fayetteville, North Carolina. At the Neuse River, Lederer changed course again, this time northward, and skirted present-day Rocky Mount, North Carolina, before reaching his final destination at Fort Henry (Petersburg), Virginia.

During this second expedition, Lederer passed through the domains of several Indian tribes, among them the Saponi, Eno, Shakori, Catawba, and Tuscarora. While visiting with a Tuscarora chief, the explorer later recalled, "His grim Majestie, upon my first appearance, demanded my Gun and Shot; which I willingly parted with, to ransom my self out of his clutches: for he was the most proud imperious Barbarian that I met with in all my Marches." Taking the Indian's hostility as a cue, Lederer determined to terminate the expedition and head for home, "where I was not a little overjoyed to see Christian faces again."

The persistent German attempted one more time to find a pass through the Appalachian Mountains and a possible connection with the Orient. On August 20, 1670, in the company of nine mounted colonists and five local Indians, he departed Robert Talifer's plantation on the Rappahannock River and rode northwestward up that stream to its headwaters in the mountains, reaching the crest of the Blue Ridge six days later. During the outward journey, he suffered his only casualty when he "was stung in my sleep by a Mountain-spider; and had not an Indian suckt out the poyson, I had died: for receiving the hurt at the tip of one of my fingers, the venome shot up immediately into my shoulder, and so inflamed my side, that it is not possible to express my torment."

Soon recovering from his spider bite, Lederer started for home. In his book he wrote, "I being thus beyond my hopes and expectation restored to my self, we unanimously agreed to return back seeing no possibility of passing through the Mountains: and finding our Indians with our horses in the place where we left them, we rode homewards without making any further Discovery." On September 1 the weary party reached the Talifer plantation by the same route followed on the outbound trip.

Although Lederer had failed to discover a passage through the Blue Ridge Mountains, his travels and discoveries shed a great deal of light on a little-known region of America. His dealings with several regional Indian tribes gave him insight into the proper manner in which to trade with the natives. For nearby tribes, he revealed that trade goods such as cloth, axes, hoes, knives, scissors, firearms, and powder were eagerly sought by the Indians, although he was quick to warn that dealing in arms and ammunition was prohibited by English authorities. For tribes situated farther afield, he suggested that such articles as mirrors, beads, toys for the children, glass bracelets, and pictures made good trade items. In return for his efforts, he opined, a successful trader could expect an abundance of top-quality beaver, otter, wildcat, fox, deer, and raccoon pelts.

The circumstances of Lederer's life following the return from his third and final trip to the Blue Ridge Mountains are not clear. He left Virginia suddenly during the fall or winter of 1670–71 and settled in Calvert County, Maryland, where he was befriended by William Talbot, the provincial secretary. It was Talbot who was instrumental in having Lederer's accounts of his explorations published in book form. While in Maryland, Lederer was issued a commission to trade with the various Indian tribes he had come in contact with during his journeys, but if he ever participated in the fur trade with the Virginia or Carolina natives, he didn't do so for very long, since his sojourn in Maryland was a brief one.

By 1674 Lederer had moved again, this time to Connecticut, where he became the personal physician to Governor John Winthrop Jr. After a brief stay, he boarded a ship bound for his native Germany, and there he passed into the pages of history. As far as is known, the elusive physician-turned-explorer never returned to America.

EDWARD TEACH MEETS HIS MAKER

North Carolina, 1718

From 1695 to 1725, the period often called the "Golden Age of Piracy," the sea lanes off the Atlantic coast of North America were ravaged by scores of freebooters who made comfortable livings attacking and plundering other ships, both government and privately owned. One of the most notorious of these brigands was an adventurer by the name of Edward Teach (sometimes spelled Thach, Tack, or Theach), better known as Blackbeard. Teach is believed to have been born around 1680 in Bristol, England, and was a veteran of Queen Anne's War (1701–14). Following his navy service, he ended up in the West Indies.

The month after his May 1718 blockade of Charleston, South Carolina, during which time he terrorized the town's citizenry, Teach elected to exercise a right extended by the King of England to forgive any and all privateers who surrendered and renounced piracy. The pirate and his crew, aboard the ship *Adventure,* entered Pamlico Sound and proceeded up the waterway to the small town of Bath, located in present-day Beaufort County. There, in an interview with

North Carolina's royal governor, Charles Eden, Teach received his pardon. The pirate was so taken aback by the beauty of the town that he decided to settle there, purchasing a house near the governor's residence and becoming an accepted member of town society. Soon afterwards, Teach married his fourteenth wife, the wedding ceremony being performed by none other than the governor himself.

Teach soon became bored with his relatively sedentary life in Bath and, before long, the high seas called to him once again. Leaving the North Carolina town, he and his fellows visited Philadelphia, where, to his surprise, a warrant had been issued for his arrest. Quickly departing the city, the pirates sailed again along the Atlantic coast before returning to North Carolina and entering Ocracoke Inlet, where they decided to take refuge for a while.

Meanwhile, Alexander Spotswood, Virginia's royal lieutenant governor and commander-in-chief of the colony, became increasingly upset that Teach and other pirates appeared to be receiving "favored status" from the governor of North Carolina and decided to do something about it. He dispatched two leased sloops, under the command of Lieutenant Robert Maynard, to sail to Ocracoke Inlet and the vicinity of Bath, where Teach and his crew were reported to be. Simultaneously, Captain Ellis Brand was sent overland to rendezvous with Maynard at Bath. Maynard set sail from present-day Hampton, Virginia, at 3:00 p.m. on November 17, while Brand departed that evening.

On November 22 Maynard and his two sloops encountered Teach in Ocracoke Inlet, just off the coast of Ocracoke Island. Teach attempted to lure Maynard's two ships onto a sandbar, hoping to strand them while he made good his escape. Failing at this, the pirate ordered his crew to open fire on the two Virginia sloops, and the barrage nearly disabled both. Several of each crew were killed and the ships damaged. When Teach ordered his men to board the sloops,

Maynard's surviving sailors fought with a vengeance in deadly hand-to-hand combat. Maynard himself wrote the following description of the battle:

> I sail'd from Virginia the 17th past [November], with
> two Sloops, and 54 Men under my Command, having
> no Guns [cannon], but only small Arms and Pistols.
> Mr. Hyde commanded the little Sloop with 22 Men,
> and I had 32 in my sloop. The 22d I came up with
> Captain Teach, the notorious Pyrate, who has taken,
> from time to time, a great many English Vessels on
> these Coasts, and in the West-Indies; he went by the
> name of Blackbeard, because he let his beard grow, and
> tied it up in black Ribbons. I attack'd him at Cherhock
> in North Carolina, when he had on Board 21 Men,
> and nine Guns mounted. At our first Salutation, he
> drank Damnation to me and my Men, whom he stil'd
> [styled] Cowardly Puppies, saying, He would neither
> give nor take Quarter. Immediately we engag'd, and
> Mr. Hyde was unfortunately kill'd, and five of his Men
> wounded in the little Sloop, which, having no-body
> to command her, fell a-stern, and did not come up to
> assist me till the Action was almost over. In the mean
> time, continuing the Fight, it being a perfect Calm
> . . . I boarded his Sloop, and had 20 Men kill'd and
> wounded. Immediately thereupon, he enter'd me with
> 10 Men; but 12 stout Men I left there, fought like
> Heroes, Sword in Hand, and they kill'd every one of

them that enter'd, without the loss of one Man on their
Side, but they were miserably cut and mangled. In the
whole, I had eight Men killed, and 18 wounded. We
kill'd 12, besides Blackbeard, who fell with five Shot in
him, and 20 dismal Cuts in several Parts of his Body.
I took nine Prisoners, mostly Negroes, all wounded. I
have cut Blackbeard's head off, which I have put on my
Bowspright, in order to carry it to Virginia. I should
never have taken him, if I had not got him in such a
Hole, whence he could not get out, for we had no Guns
[cannon] on Board; so that the engagement on our Side
was the more Bloody and Desperate.

Captain Brand reached Bath the evening of November 23, the day following the great battle at Ocracoke, and waited there for the victorious Lieutenant Maynard to join him. The Virginians discovered in the area a great quantity of sugar, indigo, cocoa, and cotton, which they sent home and sold at auction for more than 2,200 pounds sterling. The two officers remained in the vicinity of Bath for several weeks, taking care of the wounded and mending the sloops. Fifteen of Teach's compatriots, as well as the pirate's head, were returned to Williamsburg, where they were publicly displayed.

On November 24, 1718, with the blessing of the General Assembly at Williamsburg, Lieutenant Governor Spotswood issued a proclamation that outlined and described "rewards given for apprehending, or killing Pyrates." In the document, released to the public two days after Teach had been killed, Spotswood declared that bounty money was available for anyone capturing or killing a pirate or pirates within the period between November 14, 1718, and November 14, 1719, provided that such pirate or pirates were apprehended or killed between thirty-four and thirty-nine degrees of North Latitude, and within one hundred leagues of Virginia's shoreline, or within the colonies of Virginia or North Carolina. Edward Teach was the only culprit specifically named in the proclamation, and the reward for his capture or death was one hundred pounds.

With the presentation of Captain Teach's head to Spotswood by Maynard, it can be assumed that the reward money was gladly dispensed from the Virginia public treasury.

THE REAL STORY OF EVANGELINE

Louisiana, 1764

As the 1750s opened, conflicting claims between Great Britain and France over ownership of North America—home to nearly one million British and around fifty thousand French subjects—were growing more numerous and vocal. The two giant European powers found themselves on a collision course that came to a head with the outbreak of the French and Indian War in July 1754. For the next six years, vicious fighting occurred in the backwoods of America—combat that not only pitted Great Britain and its American colonial allies against France and its Canadian followers, but also divided the loyalties of many Indian tribes that eventually were forced to take one side or the other in the conflict. Another effect of the hostilities was the forced eviction by the British government of thousands of people called Acadians from their ancient homes in Canada to new locations all over America, including Louisiana.

In April 1764 a shipload of these Acadians arrived at the dock in New Orleans, vowing to begin a new life. Ten months later, some of the group's former Canadian neighbors arrived, and they were soon followed by yet more emigrants. Before the resettlement was over, nearly three thousand Acadians had moved to various locations in Louisiana and planted new roots.

These frightened sojourners came from the present-day sea-swept provinces of Nova Scotia and New Brunswick, both of which, even before the war, were British colonies. They had migrated there from France in the seventeenth century and were simple farmers who practiced Catholicism, were totally self-sufficient, and were quick to lay aside provisions for a rainy day. A visitor among the Acadians in 1750 described the friendly, pastoral people as

> *the most innocent and virtuous people whom I have ever known or heard tell of in any history. They live in a state of perfect equality, without distinction of rank in society. . . . Ignorant of the luxuries and even of the conveniences of life, they are content with a simple mode of life, which they easily derive from the cultivation of their lands. Very little ambition or avarice was seen among them; they helped each other's wants with benevolent liberality; they required no interest for loans of money or other property. They were humane and hospitable to strangers, and very liberal to those who embraced their religion. They were very remarkable for the inviolable purity of their morals. I do not recollect a single case of illegitimate births among them, even now. Their knowledge of agriculture was very limited, although they cultivated their dyked lands pretty well. . . . They were a strong, healthy people, capable of enduring great hardship, and generally lived to an*

advanced age, although no one employed a doctor. The men worked hard in planting and at harvest time and the season when the dykes were to be made or repaired, and on any occasion when work was pressing. They thus secured for half the year, at least, leisure which they spent in parties and merrymakings, of which they were very fond. . . . [R]eally, if there be a people who recall the Golden Age as described in history, it was the old-time Acadians.

Early in the war, the British king had issued a proclamation to the Acadians in Canada demanding "that your Land & Tennements, Cattle of all Kinds and Livestocks of all Sorts [be] forfeited to the Crown [but that] . . . all other . . . effects savings your money and Household Goods, and you yourselves [are] to be removed from this Province."

When noted American poet and writer Henry Wadsworth Longfellow heard about this story at a dinner party he was attending with his friend, Nathaniel Hawthorne, he was totally enthralled. Arguably nineteenth-century America's preeminent literary figure, Longfellow was born on February 27, 1807, in Portland, Maine (at the time, a part of Massachusetts), one of seven children born to Zilpah Wadsworth, daughter of a Revolutionary War general, and Stephen Longfellow, a graduate of Harvard and a practicing attorney. Henry was educated locally until he attended Bowdoin College, teaching there as well as at Harvard University following graduation.

The tale Longfellow heard at the dinner party was more than a sad story of forced exile of an innocent people; it also was the wonderful saga of two star-struck, just-married lovers named Evangeline and Gabriel, who, along with hundreds of other Acadians, were destined to wander aimlessly for years before relocating to various American colonies, Europe, and Spanish Louisiana. Intrigued by the tale, Longfellow researched it and, in 1847, produced the epic poem *Evangeline,* which told the story of the pair as they became separated in their flight from Canada and unsuccessfully searched for each other for years to come. Through the device of fiction, Longfellow had both Evangeline and Gabriel separately gravitating to Louisiana shortly after leaving Canada, and in his day, a prompt arrival there seemed reasonable. More modern research, however, has shown that nearly ten years elapsed between the Acadians' expulsion and their first arriving in New Orleans, primarily because the migrants were originally sent to other colonies.

Today, Louisiana's Cajun people proudly point to the exiled Acadians as their ancestors.

THE EDENTON TEA PARTY

North Carolina, 1774

There are few Americans who have not heard of the Boston Tea Party of December 1773, in which a group of angry Massachusetts revolutionaries dressed as Indians boarded three British ships moored in Boston Harbor and pitched 342 cases of fine English tea valued at 18,000 pounds sterling into the depths of the bay. The episode was prompted when Parliament passed the Tea Act the previous April, which cut the duties, but retained the taxes, on British tea imported by the American colonies, effectively cutting the price of imported tea and undermining the competition.

A similar and equally interesting event, though not so well publicized, occurred in Edenton, North Carolina, less than one year later. It all began when the Provincial Deputies of North Carolina, in response to the passage of the Tea Act, issued an edict forbidding the importation of British tea and cloth. In a show of women's support for the deputies, Penelope Barker, wife of the colony's royal treasurer, assembled about fifty of her friends and fellow tea drinkers on October 25, 1774, and urged them not only to refrain from using

English tea, clothes, or any other item with an English origin, but also to sign a petition that confirmed their position. The document read in part:

> *The Provincial Deputies of North Carolina, having resolved not to drink any more tea, nor wear any more British cloth, many ladies of this province have determined to give memorable proof of their patriotism, and have accordingly entered into the following honourable and spirited association. I send it to you to shew your fair countrywomen, how zealously and faithfully, American ladies follow the laudable example of their husbands, and what opposition your matchless Ministers may expect to receive from a people thus firmly united against them. . . . We cannot be indifferent on any occasion that appears nearly to affect the peace and happiness of our country, and . . . it is a duty which we owe, not only to our near and dear connections . . . but to ourselves.*

Word of the Edenton ladies' tea party and petition-signing was slow getting to England, but when the news did arrive, it was met with a combination of surprise, consternation, and amusement. On the one hand, women—especially those living in the colonies— were not expected to express their opinions on any type of matter, much less highly volatile, political issues. A North Carolina royalist, Arthur Iredell, was visiting London when the sober tidings from America arrived, and in a caustic letter to his brother back home, he chided, "If the Ladies, who have ever since the Amazonian Era, been esteemed the most formidable Enemies, if they, I say, should attack us, the most fatal consequence is to be dreaded," adding that "each wound they give is mortal. . . . The more we try to conquer them, the more we are conquered."

About five months after the Edenton tea party, ladies in the North Carolina port town of Wilmington, some 150 miles to the south, staged a similar, but more active, demonstration. Little documentation remains about the Wilmington affair, and the exact details have become lost over the years. However, apparently following editorials in the *South Carolina Gazette,* a Charleston newspaper that advocated a public outcry against the Tea Act and other unpopular British edicts, Wilmington women renounced the tea-drinking habit and actually burned their tea supplies. A Scotswoman, visiting America at the time, later wrote scathingly, "They had delayed however till the sacrifice was not very considerable, as I do not think any one offered [to burn] above a quarter of a pound."

History has failed to record what effect, if any, the Edenton and Wilmington tea parties had upon the British government during those final days before the outbreak of revolution, as officials planned to invade the American colonies and, through force of arms, demand the loyalties of its wayward subjects. What is known is that when the ladies of Edenton signed their names to the petition decrying British wrongs, they became one of the first groups of women in America, if not *the* first, to collectively make their feelings and desires known to a higher political authority.

JAMES ADAIR'S SOJOURN
IN ALABAMA

Alabama, 1775

For at least the past fifty years, most anthropologists have agreed that the first Americans crossed the frozen Bering land bridge connecting Siberia with Alaska on foot, and, over centuries, drifted southward to populate both North and South America. Today, this portrait of colonization of the New World is under heavy fire as more and more archaeological sites are being discovered containing evidence of human habitation that predates the earlier scenario by thousands of years. American anthropology and archaeology are at a crisis, with several theories on the early peopling of the continent in vogue—including one that has early Europeans utilizing an Atlantic ice bridge from east to west across the ocean to the eastern coasts of Canada and the United States.

This current spirited controversy brings to mind similar arguments about the origin of the American Indians debated hundreds of years ago, well before modern science supposedly put the issue to rest. One of the most popular theories, dating as far back as 1607, was that New World natives were descended from the famed Lost Tribes of Israel. The author of that early theory, a Catholic priest, confused the issue even more when he introduced several other possibilities vying for the honor of being the progenitor of the Indians, postulating that:

> *The Indians proceed neither from one nation or people, nor have they come from one part alone of the Old World, or by the same road, or at the same time, in the same way, or for the same reasons; some have probably descended from the Carthaginians, others from the Ten Lost Tribes and other Israelites, others from the lost Atlantis, from the Greeks, and Phoenicians, and still others from the Chinese, Tartars, and other groups.*

Over the years the "Lost Tribes of Israel" theory became very popular among parlor historians and scientists alike, and no one researched the subject better or documented it with more authority than an English trader among the Alabama Indians. His name was James Adair and he was a socially prominent, well-educated Irishman born in County Antrim in about 1709. In 1735 he migrated to Charles Town (present-day Charleston), South Carolina, and for the next forty years traveled, resided with, and became a staunch friend, supporter, and advocate of the Catawba, Cherokee, Muscogee (Creek), Choctaw, and Chickasaw tribes who lived across the southeastern part of the country.

Adair eventually wrote a monumental book, *The History of the American Indians, Particularly Those Nations Adjoining to the Mississippi, East and West Florida, Georgia* [including, of course, most of present-day Alabama], *South and North Carolina, and Virginia,* the first half of which sets forth twenty-two arguments why he believes American Indians were descended from the Ten Lost Tribes of Israel. They range from similarities between the two people's division into tribes, to their manner of counting time, the burial of their dead, and their laws of uncleanness. Actually, this makes for tedious reading, especially since there is no scientific justification for the bizarre theory to begin with.

The second half of the book is another matter altogether. In these pages, Adair, the intellectual and trader, has produced an encyclopedia that covers the lifestyles, habits, hunting methods, architecture, dress, agricultural pursuits, and more of several of the most important Indian tribes in the Old South before they were influenced by white encroachment.

Of Alabama's natives, Adair wrote that the region in which they lived was "called the Creek country, on account of the great number of Creeks, or small bays, rivulets, and swamps, it abounds with," adding:

> *This nation is generally computed to consist of about 3500 men fit to bear arms; and has fifty towns, or villages. . . . Most of their towns are very commodiously and pleasantly situated, on large, beautiful creeks, or rivers, where the lands are fertile, the water clear and well tasted, and the air extremely pure. . . . The nation consists of a mixture of several broken tribes [meaning, otherwise, unattached to each other], whom the Muskohge [Muscogee] artfully decoyed to incorporate with them, in order to strengthen themselves against hostile attempts.*

And, Adair reported, this strengthening of their nation yielded results. According to the trader, "They [the Creek] are certainly the most powerful Indian nation we are acquainted with on this continent, and within thirty years past, they are grown very warlike."

During Adair's sojourn among the Alabama Creeks, the French military maintained an outpost, Fort Toulouse, north of present-day Montgomery, near the confluence of the Tallapoosa and Coosa Rivers. The trader was less than complimentary of the French, citing their use of "corrupting brandy, taffy, and decoying trifles" to imbue "false notions of the ill intentions of our [English] colonies." The "conduct of the Christian French," he declared, "has fixed many of the Muskohge in a strong native hatred to the British Americans," which would only increase "unless we give them such a severe lesson, as their annual conduct to us has highly deserved since the year 1760." As future events proved, however, it was not the English who gave the Creeks their "severe lesson," but rather Americans and Cherokee allies commanded by Andrew Jackson during several decisive victories in Alabama during 1813–14.

During the years 1761–68, while a guest of the Chickasaw tribe, Adair wrote a large portion of his anticipated book. He left his beloved Southern Indian friends in 1768, traveling to New York to meet with the English Indian agent Sir William Johnson. On September 7, 1769, the *South Carolina Gazette* carried news of the proposed book, publishing an article in which it was stated:

> *An account of the origin of the primitive inhabit-*
> *ants and a history of those numerous warlike tribes of*
> *Indians, situated to the westward of Charles Town*
> *are subjects hitherto unattempted by any pen. . . .*
> *Such an attempt has [now] been made by Mr. James*

Adair, a gentleman who has been conversant among the Cherokees, Chickesaws [sic], Choctaws, etc., for thirty-odd years past; and who, by the assistance of a liberal education, a long experience among them and a genius naturally formed for curious enquiries, has written essays on their origin, language, religion, customary methods of making war and peace, etc.

Adair's whereabouts are unknown for the next six years or so—between the time the newspaper told of his upcoming book and the date (1775) the book was actually published in London—although the 1769 article did report that the trader-turned-author would soon be departing for England to meet with prospective publishers. In any event, the book did appear in London bookstalls in 1775 and was well received by the English reading public. In 1782, following its London debut, a German edition was released in Breslau. From then until 1930, when Tennessee historian and state supreme court judge Samuel Cole Williams published an edited and annotated edition, it was never reissued. A testament to the current importance of Adair as historian and of the book as solid history lies in the fact that the volume has been in continuous print for the past forty years.

THE COURT-MARTIAL
OF DANIEL BOONE

Kentucky, 1778

Ask any number of history buffs for the name of the one historical figure who most embodies the American frontier, and it is highly likely that an overwhelming majority will respond, "Daniel Boone." Yet few people, other than the most astute historians, are aware that this icon of the country's early pioneer spirit was once court-martialed for treason by his fellow Kentucky associates.

Boone's legal problems began in January 1778, when he and his neighbors at Boonesborough in present-day Kentucky found themselves running out of food and other provisions, especially salt, an element important to the settlers in the curing of meat. On January 1 Boone and several men from the fort, which was situated on the middle stretch of the Kentucky River, traveled northeast to Blue Licks, located some thirty miles away on the Licking River. There, Boone figured, a few weeks of gathering the salt water from the Licks and boiling it in huge kettles until the liquid evaporated would yield many pounds of the much-needed salt.

For close to five weeks, Boone's twenty-seven companions labored at the springs extracting salt from the brine. Boone himself, rather than working with the salt makers, decided instead to become the party's hunter, and it was he who was responsible for bringing in the meat to feed his hungry fellows. By February 7 it was decided that the several hundred pounds of salt that had been distilled was sufficient to last through the winter, and the group began to make plans to return home.

In the meantime, nearby in the woods, Boone had just killed a buffalo and was loading the meat onto his horse when he found himself surrounded by four Shawnee Indian braves. The quick-witted frontiersman, four days short of his forty-third birthday, made a run for it, but the speedy young warriors soon overtook and captured him. "I was taken prisoner by a party of Shaney Indians," the resolute Boone later recalled.

Most of the Shawnee towns were located on the north side of the Ohio River, but hunting and war parties often crossed the stream into Kentucky. Boone soon discovered that his four captors were part of Chief Blackfish's group, which had only recently arrived in the area. He also learned that it was Blackfish's intent to attack Boonesborough in retaliation for the recent murder of his friend and fellow chief, Cornstalk, by Virginia militia members while the Shawnee leader was being held prisoner.

When Boone was escorted to the main Shawnee camp, Chief Blackfish revealed to him his plans to destroy Boonesborough as well as to kill Boone and his salt-gatherers. The quick-thinking Boone convinced the chief that it would be to his advantage to wait until spring to attack Boonesborough, at which time he would personally convince his fellow settlers to peaceably surrender. In the meantime, the frontiersman volunteered to surrender himself and his companions and to accompany their Shawnee captors back to Ohio.

Boone, his companions, and the large Shawnee war party soon arrived in Chillicothe (today's community of Oldtown, located a few miles east of Dayton, Ohio). For the next several months, Boone lived as the adopted son of Blackfish, taking the name Sheltowee, or "Big Turtle." During his residency at Chillicothe, he visited Detroit and had an interview with the British lieutenant governor, Henry Hamilton, assuring him that he would persuade his fellow Kentuckians to surrender to the Shawnees and to throw their support to the British.

Soon after Boone's return to Chillicothe, a fellow Kentuckian named Andy Johnson escaped from his Shawnee captors and made it across the Ohio River to Harrodsburg. There, Johnson told Boone's neighbors and close associates of their friend's bizarre behavior among the Indians and his supposed treasonous acts of consorting with the enemy. Johnson declared that Boone was a Tory, adding that he "had surrendered them all up to the British, and taken the oath of allegiance to the British at Detroit." When the news spread, all of Kentucky was shocked, that was until June 20, 1778, the day old Daniel showed up at the gate at Boonesborough, looking more like an Indian than he did a white man.

Boone quickly apprised the fort's residents of the impending Shawnee attack and explained to them that had he not played along with the Indians' plans, they would have all been killed months earlier. The fort was strengthened, water and supplies were stored, and preparations were made for a long siege. When no attackers appeared over the next few weeks, Boone led a small command across the Ohio River, ran into a party of Shawnees, gave fight, and quickly returned to Boonesborough.

On September 7 nearly five hundred Shawnees—led by an irate Blackfish and accompanied by a few British soldiers—arrived at Boonesborough demanding the fort's surrender. An unarmed Boone and several defenders left the safety of the stockade to parley with the enemy. When a few Indians attempted to capture Boone and the other men, the fort's defenders fired upon them, allowing Daniel and the others to escape. For the next nine days, the enemy force tried every ploy to overtake Boonesborough's less-than-sixty-man garrison, including the digging of an elaborate tunnel network whereby they hoped to undermine the fort. Only an unrelenting rain which caved in the tunnels, coupled with the attackers' own fatigue, saved the settlers. On the morning of September 17, the Shawnees and their British allies called off the attack and returned across the Ohio.

Shortly after the siege at Boonesborough, Colonel Richard Callaway preferred charges against Boone and convinced militia authorities to hold a court-martial. Logan's Station, situated twenty-five miles southwest of Boonesborough, was the site of the trial. The proceedings started with Callaway's accusations that Boone's true intention for surrendering his men at Blue Licks was to "give up all the people of Boonesborough" and to "live under British jurisdiction." An eyewitness at the trial, Daniel Trabue, gave Boone's version of the events, writing years later:

> *Capt. Daniel Boon [sic] sayed the reason he give up*
> *these men at the blue licks was that the Indeans told*
> *him they was going to Boonesborough to take the fort.*
> *Boon said he thought he would use some stratigem.*
> *He thought the fort was in bad order and the Indeans*
> *would take it easy. He (Boon) said he told the Indi-*
> *ans the fort was very strong and too many men for*
> *them, that he was friendly to them (and the officers at*
> *Detroyt) and he would go and shew them some men—*
> *to wit, 26—and he would go with them to Detroyt*
> *and these men also, and when they come to take*

*Boonesborough they must have more warriers than they
now had. Boon said he told them all these tails to fool
them. He also said he Did tell the British officers he
would be friendly to them and try to give up Boonsbor-
ough but that he was a trying to fool them.*

Boone's careful recollection of the past year's events and his per-
suasive manner quickly convinced the members of the court-martial
that his every deed had been in the best interests of Boonesborough
and its residents. His ploy to cooperate with the Shawnees was the
only way he could have worked his way out of the predicament he
and his men found themselves in at Blue Licks, and the surrender
and removal of the prisoners to Ohio had only bought extra time
for the Kentuckians to get ready for battle. Colonel Callaway's arguments crumbled before the strong case that Boone presented in his
own defense.

Boone was acquitted of all charges and promoted to major of
the militia. With this unsavory experience now behind him, he
soon headed for North Carolina to retrieve his wife and family,
who had returned there on the assumption that he had been killed
by the Shawnees.

THE BATTLE OF KINGS MOUNTAIN

South Carolina, 1780

By 1778 the Revolutionary War's main theater had shifted to the South. Whereas all of the previous major battles had been waged in Massachusetts, New York, New Jersey, or Pennsylvania, following the Battle of Monmouth in New Jersey in June 1778, nine of the last ten most important engagements occurred in the Carolinas, Georgia, and Virginia. In December 1778, British forces occupied Savannah, Georgia, and during the following October, American forces failed to retake the important seaport. Charleston, South Carolina, fell to the British on May 12, 1780, and by mid-August the British had also won an important victory at Camden, South Carolina.

Although the Revolution is usually thought of as being a war waged between ragtag American colonists and a well-disciplined, uniformed British army, it is interesting to note that at the time the conflict began in 1775, about one-third of all colonists maintained a rabid loyalty to the Crown and were not interested in breaking the bonds between America and King George III. Consequently, many battles in the South—where those loyalties to royalty persisted well into the war—were fought brother against brother and American against American.

On October 25, 1780, Elizabeth Maxwell Steel, a resident of Salisbury, North Carolina, wrote an encouraging letter to a friend:

> *With the utmost satisfaction I can acquaint you with the sudden and favorable turn of our public affairs. A few days ago destruction hung over our heads. Cornwallis with at least 1500 British and Tories waited at Charlotte for the reinforcement of 1000 from Broad River, which reinforcement has been entirely cut off, 130 killed and the remainder captured. Cornwallis immediately retreated, and is now on his way toward Charleston, with part of our army in his rear.*

Mrs. Steele was describing news of the recent events at Kings Mountain, South Carolina, where eighteen days earlier a large contingent of American Whig (patriot) troops—consisting primarily of backwoodsmen from Virginia, the Carolinas, and present-day Tennessee (at the time, still a part of North Carolina)—had mercilessly defeated an army of American Tories (loyalists) under the command of British Major Patrick Ferguson.

Kings Mountain is located just south of the North Carolina border a few miles east of what is now Spartanburg and, when viewed from a distance, displays many of the same properties it possessed on that long-ago October day in 1780. Jutting into the air several hundred feet above the surrounding relatively flat countryside, the mountain should have been avoided by Ferguson as a place to wage battle against fierce frontiersmen. What the commander failed to consider, however, and no doubt a point that placed him in extreme harm, was the fact that his enemy was trained in so-called Indian warfare—hit and run, duck behind trees and rocks, almost guerilla-like action—whereas he had trained his Tory allies to fight in classic British army formation, where one rank of soldiers fired and then dropped to the ground while ranks behind them fired, and so forth. Deploying his troops at the very peak of the mountain, he and his command did not stand a chance when confronted by the Appalachian frontiersmen, thirsty for blood.

As both armies positioned themselves, one of the patriot commanders, Colonel Benjamin Cleveland, addressed the men in his unit as follows:

> *My brave fellows, every man must consider himself an officer, and act from his own judgment. Fire as quickly as you can, and stand your ground as long as you can. When you can do no better, get behind trees, or retreat; but I beg you not to run quite off if we are repulsed, let us make a point of returning and renewing the fight; perhaps we may have better luck in the second attempt than in the first.*

If someone could have magically observed the battle from the air, that person would have noticed that Kings Mountain looked like a gigantic cooking spoon, long and narrow on the southwestern end like the spoon's handle, and widening on the northeastern end into the spoon itself. Ferguson placed his troops along the entire length of the spoon—along the highest elevation—while the patriots completely surrounded him at lower elevations. Ferguson had no place to go, but again, thinking that the patriots would fight in the classic European fashion, this bothered him little. He boasted that he "was on Kings Mountain, that he was king of the Mountain, and God Almighty could not drive him from it."

As Ferguson predicted, God Almighty did not drive him from Kings Mountain, but the riflemen from Tennessee, Virginia, and the Carolinas did. In the confusion of the battle, Ferguson allowed his command to become totally enveloped by the patriot army, and when the fighting was over, sixty-five minutes after it began, his Tories had suffered 119 men killed, 123 wounded, and 664 captured. The patriots had twenty-eight men killed and sixty-two wounded. Ferguson himself was mortally wounded by patriot rifle fire as he rode back and forth attempting to marshal his troops.

The American Whig victory at Kings Mountain was truly a decisive—if not *the* decisive—turning point of the Revolutionary War in the South. Thousands of Tories who maintained their loyalties to the Crown stood aghast at the sudden and total defeat of their allies, while the British commander, Lieutenant General Charles Lord Cornwallis, was forced to retreat.

In the ensuing publicity about the victory of the American rebels over the Tories, many contemporary ballads were written, among them one titled "Ferguson's Defeat." Following are two of its twelve stanzas:

> *We laid old Ferguson dead on the ground,*
> *Four hundred and fifty dead Tories lay round—*
> *Making a large escort, if not quite so wise,*
> *To guide him to his chosen abode in the skies. . . .*

> *We shouted the victory that we did obtain,*
> *Our voices were heard seven miles on the plain,*
> *Liberty shall stand—and the Tories shall fall,*
> *Here's an end to my song, so God bless you all!*

On March 15, 1781, less than six months after Patrick Ferguson's defeat by the backwoodsmen at Kings Mountain, patriot forces commanded by Generals Nathanael Greene and Daniel Morgan engaged the British army, led by General Cornwallis, at Guilford Courthouse, North Carolina. Although technically the confrontation was a victory for the British, Cornwallis's army was so badly mauled that the action left the Crown's army in the South in an extremely delicate position for its final campaign in Virginia the following autumn. There, on the banks of the York River, on October 19, 1781, the infant United States finally realized its independence when Cornwallis surrendered to General George Washington's forces after several days of intense combat. It was Britain's defeat at Yorktown, Virginia, preceded by the debacle at Kings Mountain, that dashed all hopes of the Crown retaining a colonial empire in North America.

THE INVENTION OF
THE COTTON GIN

Georgia, 1792

If anyone was ever down on his luck, it was surely twenty-six-year-old Eli Whitney. Sitting on the veranda of Mrs. Nathanael Greene's beautiful plantation home, Mulberry Grove, located just outside Savannah, Georgia, Whitney contemplated the chain of events that had brought him, a Massachusetts "Yankee," to the Deep South. He had graduated from Yale College only a few months earlier and had been lured to Georgia in anticipation of filling a tutoring position that promised to pay well enough to get him out of the large debt he had incurred putting himself through school. But, alas, when he arrived, he learned that his employer intended to pay him only half of the previously agreed-upon salary. The kindhearted Mrs. Greene, widow of the famed Revolutionary War general, insisted that he stay on her plantation until he could find more work.

It was a hot summer's day in 1792, and Whitney and Phineas Miller, Mrs. Greene's caretaker, were discussing ideas that might make the two young men money. Miller was also interested in a project that would help Mrs. Greene recover from the heavy debt that she had incurred trying to operate her large, but only marginally profitable, plantation. The subject soon turned to cotton.

Cotton had just recently found itself in large demand in England for the manufacture of fine cloth. However, the variety that was grown in Georgia and neighboring states—and the type that could be easily processed by machine—only grew in the lowlands near the ocean, and the production of marketable quantities was very limited. Whitney was told that another kind of cotton, "short-staple," was an easy grower anywhere in the warm, moist climes of the South. The only problem with the short-staple variety was the extreme difficulty in separating the seeds from the fiber. The machine used for the other variety was of no use on short-staple cotton, and consequently, short-staple required one person's labor for a full day to produce one pound of marketable, seed-free cotton. If only someone could come up with a device to automatically remove the seeds from the fiber, the growing of cotton could bring an economic boon to farmers all over the region.

That day on Mrs. Greene's sprawling front porch was a turning point in Eli Whitney's life. The young teacher was excited about the conversations he had with Miller and other discussions like them with various plantation owners and overseers in the region. During the next few weeks, the notion that there must be some easy, inexpensive way to extract the cottonseeds from the fiber preyed on his mind. Finally, after hours of daydreaming and trial-and-error design work, he produced a prototype cotton gin that performed the desired functions without a hitch. Explaining to his father the chain of events that had occurred since he arrived in Georgia, the contented inventor wrote:

> *There were a number of very respectable gentle-*
> *men . . . who all agreed that if a machine could be*

*invented which would gin the cotton with expedition,
it would be a great thing both to the country and to the
inventor. In about ten days I made a little model, for
which I was offered, if I would give up all right and
title to it, a Hundred Guineas. I concluded to relinquish my school and turn my attention to perfecting
the machine. I made one . . . with which one man will
clean ten times as much cotton as he can in any other
way before known.*

Whitney and Miller soon became partners and told the nearby
Georgia landowners that their goal was to build enough cotton gins
to place them at convenient places throughout the region, thus allowing a grower to bring in his cotton, have it processed, and pay for
the processing with a share of the "clean" fiber. Now, amid glowing
success, a serious problem arose: The demand for the new machines
outgrew the ability of the two men to build them. Whitney returned
to New England, where he hired skilled labor to manufacture the
gins en masse, while Miller stayed in Georgia to handle the administrative and logistical aspects of the new partnership.

It soon occurred to Whitney that his cotton gin, as revolutionary
as it was, would be extremely easy to reproduce if some unscrupulous
person had the notion. The partners had been careful not to divulge
details of the design to anyone, and even refused to allow cotton
growers to watch the gin while it processed their cotton. Accordingly,
in June 1793, Whitney applied for a patent on his machine. In the
application he proudly wrote, "That with the Ginn, if turned with
horses or by water, two persons will clean enough cotton in one day,
as a hundred persons could clean in the same time with ginns now
in common use."

More problems were to beset Miller and Whitney, as the new company was called. In March 1795 fire destroyed the New Haven, Connecticut, factory where the cotton gins were manufactured. A disheartened but resolute Whitney ruefully declared:

> *For more than two years, I have spared no pains nor exertion to systematize and arrange my business in a proper manner. This object I have just accomplished. It was the purchase of many a toilsome day and sleepless night. But my prospects are all blasted and my labor lost. I do not, however, despair and I hope I shall not sink under my misfortune. I shall reestablish the business as soon as possible but it must be a long time before I can repair my loss.*

As things turned out, Whitney never "repaired" his loss. Struggling to recover from the severe damages—both emotional and economic—caused by the fire, he watched helplessly as dozens of counterfeit cotton gins flooded the marketplace. His only recourse was to go to court, and before the ordeal was over, he had sixty lawsuits pending against those who had stolen his design. All of his erstwhile efforts, however, were to little avail. Although the state of South Carolina, after years of delay, finally awarded him a settlement of $50,000, authorities in Georgia denied that he was the inventor of the cotton gin in the first place! The final straw came when the U.S. Congress, spearheaded by several of its Southern members, refused Whitney the right to renew his patent when the original registration expired.

Whitney finally threw in the towel. The fire that destroyed his New Haven factory, the endless lawsuits—most of them ruled against him—and the tremendous debt that he and his partner had acquired in pursuit of their business proved to be too much for the men to continue. Whitney never returned to Georgia, turning his attentions instead to the plausibility of mass-producing firearms, a business that eventually made him a wealthy man.

Despite Whitney's failure to garner personal success from the invention of the cotton gin, his accomplishment caused such an impact on the South that cotton soon became the entire region's number one cash crop. Less than 200,000 pounds of cotton were exported in 1791, when the tedious work of separating the plant's seeds from the fiber was still largely performed by hand. A dozen years later, Southern growers were selling forty-one million pounds of cotton a year, and the plant had become the basis for the "plantation" economy that had spread over much of the South in the days before the Civil War.

EARLY INDIAN TRADE IN GEORGIA

Georgia, 1796

In 1795 a remote spot in the swamplands of extreme Southeastern Georgia was selected by the United States government to become one of two sites to implement an ambitious project. It was called the "Factory System" and, before its demise almost thirty years later, it oversaw the operation of a number of trading posts located all over the region east of the Mississippi River, as well as a few in the trans-Mississippi West.

President George Washington realized the need for an Indian policy that would bring the tribes under the influence of the infant United States government, and fulfilling the day-to-day needs of the friendly tribes appeared to be a good way to accomplish the mission. As early as 1793, in one of his messages to Congress, Washington had strongly suggested that "the establishment of commerce with the Indian nations, on behalf of the United States, is most likely to conciliate their attachment," but added that "it [the trade] ought to be conducted without fraud, without extortion, with constant and plentiful supplies, with a ready market for the commodities of the

Indians, and a stated price for what they give in payment and receive in exchange."

The president's plea fell on deaf ears. The following year he renewed his efforts to establish a meaningful trading system with the natives. "I cannot refrain from again pressing upon your deliberations the plan which I recommended at the last session for the improvement of harmony with all the Indians within our limits by the fixing and conducting of trading houses," he declared, this time prompting the formation of a House of Representatives committee to explore the possibilities of his recommendations. On March 3, 1795, after being persuaded that the Indian tribes would fall under British influence if some kind of trading system was not initiated immediately, Congress finally passed a bill approving the Factory System.

The system provided for a series of government-operated Indian stores, or factories, eventually numbering twenty-eight, to be established among various Indian tribes, mostly in frontier regions with few white settlers. The stores were stocked with all types of top-quality trade goods in which the Indians would have an interest, including rifles, powder, balls, hunting knives, hatchets, cooking pots and utensils, cloth and sewing supplies, beads, and trinkets. The Indians, in exchange for these goods, gladly swapped their furs and deer hides, both items being in high demand back East. Simply stated, the system, according to an early historian of the period, Reuben Gold Thwaites, "was an attempt to conduct the Indian trade by government agents, and to give the Indians the benefit of fair dealing, and of goods at cost price."

Had the Factory System been successful, it would have provided a vehicle for much smoother Anglo-Indian relations in the future and could have rendered the fledgling nation a source of substantial, badly needed income. The policy's eventual failure in 1822, however, not only jeopardized the homogeneity of the two races, but also left the door to the vast trans–Mississippi River fur trade open to any and all comers.

The selected site in Georgia for one of the first two factories was Colerain, located just east of Okefenokee Swamp on the north bank of the Saint Marys River, the dividing line between Georgia and Spanish Florida. The post's customers were to be the Creek Indians, a powerful Muskogean-speaking tribe whose several thousand members frequented large areas of present-day Central and Southern Georgia and Alabama, but whose closest primary villages were located a couple hundred miles away. For several years British fur traders stationed out of Pensacola, Florida, had monopolized the Creek trade, and American government officials were particularly anxious to make inroads into this potentially dangerous relationship.

When Edward Price, the newly appointed factor, or chief agent, arrived at his post at Colerain on January 11, 1796, he found it to be a little less desirable than he had been led to believe it would be. He wrote:

> *The factory consisted of a store 60 feet by 28 feet on one story, half of which had no floor in it. Soldiers had been pilfering the government goods. A strong tendency toward liquor existed among all classes. Neither corn nor any other products from the soil were to be had. It was impossible to purchase milk, vegetables, poultry or even fish. The inhabitants of the country presented a wretched appearance.*

Colerain survived only eighteen months as a government fur post, its successful performance greatly hindered by its distance from the Creek villages.

Price's relationships with the neighboring Indians had been less than stellar as well, when it occurred to him that his mind and body were not suitable to the government trader's life. Nevertheless, the disgruntled agent oversaw the relocation of the Colerain factory to a new site, Fort Wilkinson, located some 175 miles north near present-day Milledgeville. When Price died at the new location in early 1799, he was replaced by Edward Wright. Jonathan Halsted succeeded Wright in March 1802 and supervised the factory at Fort Wilkinson until September 1806, when, once again, the facility moved, this time to Fort Hawkins on the site of what is now Macon.

Throughout its tenure, the Creek factory was plagued by under-performance and poor profits. Toward the end of the 1816 trading year, the storeroom at Fort Hawkins contained only $43 worth of furs and peltries. A year later the factory was moved west to Fort Mitchell, which was located on the Chattahoochee River just across the Georgia border in Mississippi Territory (present-day Alabama). There, the factory survived only a few more years before permanently closing its gates in 1821.

The year following the closing of the Creek factory at Fort Mitch-ell, a powerful body of politicians—led by Missouri senator Thomas Hart Benton and lobbyists for large, privately owned fur corporations, especially John Jacob Astor's American Fur Company—doomed the Factory System. Benton, always an enemy of the system, strongly advocated in Congress that private companies, such as his friend Astor's American Fur, be allowed to enter the lucrative fur trade as newer and more rewarding areas of pristine wilderness were being exploited along the upper Missouri River and in the Rocky Mountains. By this late date, the Factory System was suffering from a combination of misman-agement, poor performance, and dwindling public support.

Few Americans were really surprised when they read in their newspapers that, on May 6, 1822, President James Monroe had signed the bill abolishing the Factory System. What may have astounded them—had they been familiar with all of the facts at the time—is that during the system's brief life, it had operated twenty-eight factories located throughout practically the entire eastern United States and extending more than a hundred miles west of the Mississippi River.

Hundreds of thousands, if not millions, of dollars worth of trade goods were exchanged for rich, luxuriant furs, which in turn were transported to eastern markets for processing and, in some cases, exportation to Europe. It is indeed ironic that the United States—today known throughout the world as the bulwark of capitalism and free enterprise—should have proposed, and propagated, from the nation's very beginnings a system of trade with the native population wherein total control was vested with the federal government.

AN ENGLISHMAN IN LOUISIANA

Louisiana, 1797

In early June 1797 a young Englishman named Frances Baily approached the small Louisiana village of Baton Rouge, where the Spanish commandant checked his passport and allowed him to continue his journey to New Orleans. Baily was traveling through a part of present-day Louisiana that was, at the time, still under the control of the Spanish monarchy, which had acquired the vast territory at the end of the French and Indian War when France ceded the region to Spain rather than relinquish it to Great Britain as spoils of war. Within the next few years, the United States, under the direction of President Thomas Jefferson, would acquire possession of Louisiana Territory through its purchase from France. But, for now, when Baily visited, Spain still ruled the trans-Mississippi West from the mouth of the Mississippi River all the way to the Canadian border and to the hinterlands of today's Southwest.

Frances Baily had arrived in Norfolk, Virginia, on February 14, 1796, following a nearly four-month, somewhat circuitous voyage from England through the West Indies. He had decided to journey to the United States for apparently no other reason than to see the sights and enjoy the marvels of the infant country that had declared its independence from his own nation less than a quarter century earlier. For the next two years, Baily—in addition to visiting such prominent towns as Baltimore, Philadelphia, and New York—traveled the backwoods of America, chalking up more than three thousand miles on foot and on horseback, aboard flatboat and canoe.

From his initial sojourns in the eastern seaboard towns, Baily had made his way to Pittsburgh, Pennsylvania, and his first backwoods experience. From there he traveled down the Ohio River to the Mississippi, then downstream to Baton Rouge, arriving there on June 4, 1797.

Baily and his small entourage departed Baton Rouge at sunrise the following day, bound for the fabled town of New Orleans. The Englishman kept a detailed journal of his travels—posthumously published in 1856 in London—titled *Journal of a Tour in Unsettled Parts of North America in 1796 & 1797*. Of the river trip between Baton Rouge and New Orleans, he wrote:

> *Our eyes were continually feasted by the prospect of one uninterrupted chain of plantations, scattered at unequal distances along the shore. This immense river also, which was higher here than the surrounding country, was kept from overflowing these plantations by a raised bank, called a levee, which formed a fine broad walk immediately on the border of the river, and in many places was planted with orange and lemon trees. This happy mixture of nature and art was very enchanting to the sight, particularly as it presented a scene so totally new and unlooked for by us. In this*

delightful spot, where every thing seemed to be pro-
duced without any effort of art, I could not but fancy
myself as wafted along the gentle bosom of the Nile,
and that this fertile and inundated country was in
the immediate vicinity of Grand Cairo, or some other
opulent city. I could scarcely imagine that I was on
the surface of a river which had flowed nearly 3,000
miles, and scarcely beheld the face of man, much less
washed the feet of his habitation, and that had barely
200 miles farther to go ere it would be for ever lost as a
name in the great body of the ocean.

On Tuesday, June 6, Baily and his traveling companions arrived at New Orleans, staying there a little more than two weeks. For a settlement so far removed from civilization, Baily found accommodations in the town to be quite comfortable. Soon after disembarking, he had a chance meeting with a man he had met earlier in Natchez, who invited Baily to be a guest at a nearby boardinghouse in which he and several Americans lodged. From there, the Englishman explored the town and described it at length in his journal.

He found New Orleans to be surrounded by a fortification and consisting of 105 square blocks that covered about three hundred acres, not all of which had been built upon. The town consisted of about one thousand houses and possessed a Catholic cathedral, a public square, a government house, military barracks, a market, and a convent with a large garden. But, despite the beauty of New Orleans and environs and the awesomeness of the Mississippi River, the region was regularly visited by harrowing and destructive storms, which Baily called hurricanes but which appear more to have been severe summer storms. In his journal, he wrote:

There is one thing which I must not overlook in my description of this river, and that is, the astonishing hurricanes to which you are exposed in descending it. . . . [T]o present an accurate picture of them, is far beyond the powers of description. I could not ascertain whether they always presented such awful appearances; but certain it is, that almost every night, about twelve o'clock, we were awakened by the report of the most tremendous thunder echoing from the surrounding woods, accompanied with the most vivid, dense flashes of lightning the imagination can conceive; at the same time the wind would blow with incredible fury, like a tornado; and all combined seemed to threaten our little bark with instant destruction.

Baily had originally intended to depart New Orleans by ship and sail around Florida to New York City, but when he learned that it might take weeks before a ship would become available, he decided to trek overland on horseback to Natchez in present-day Mississippi, then northward along the Natchez Trace to Nashville, Tennessee. Leaving New Orleans on June 21, Baily and his party, clothed "with a proper dress for traveling the wilderness," crossed Lake Pontchartrain and then proceeded to Natchez some two hundred miles away, arriving there six days later. From Natchez, he entered the wilderness again, this time on the nearly five-hundred-mile-long Natchez Trace, which carried him to Nashville. From Nashville, he traveled through yet another vast wilderness to Knoxville, Tennessee, and eventually made his way to New York, where he departed for England on January 28, 1798.

Upon his return to England, Baily immersed himself in the stock market, actuarial studies, writing, and eventually astronomy. He was a founder and four-time president of the Royal Astronomical Society and was twice awarded gold medals by that organization for his tireless work in the field. He died in London in 1844.

THE DEATH OF
GEORGE WASHINGTON

Virginia, 1799

On July 9, 1799, George Washington reposed at his desk in the study at Mount Vernon and wrote his last will and testament. It was a lengthy document, numbering more than five thousand words, and in it the weary Virginian waxed eloquent as he made arrangements for a vast number of bequests to family and friends.

To his wife, Martha, he would leave the "use, profit and, benefit of my whole Estate, real and personal, for the term of her natural life," excluding specific items that he designated for other individuals. He decreed that upon Martha's death, "It is my Will and desire that all the Slaves which I hold in *my own right,* shall receive their freedom," explaining that to "emancipate them during [her] life, would, tho' earnestly wished by me, be attended with . . . insuperable difficulties" with the slaves Martha owned and had brought into the marriage and over whom he had no control.

He left instructions for clothing, feeding, and educating young orphan slaves, and expressly forbade the "sale, or transportation out of said Commonwealth [Virginia], of any Slave I may die possessed of, under any pretense whatsoever." And, to William Lee, an elderly mulatto slave who had been with his master for years, he bestowed "immediate freedom" and a gift of $30 "as a testimony of my sense of his attachment to me, and for his faithful services during the Revolutionary War."

Washington had a sizable number of blood relatives and close friends and, to each of them, and to many of Martha's kin as well, he willed some item of value, from building lots in the District of Columbia to his other farms along the Potomac, and from the gold-headed walking stick given to him by Benjamin Franklin to a pair of "finely wrought steel Pistols." To his faithful secretary, Tobias Lear, he gave the use of a 360-acre farm, free of rent, until Lear's death. To each of his five nephews he left one of his valuable swords, "with an injunction not to unsheath them for the purpose of shedding blood, except it be for self defence, or in defence of their Country and its rights."

When he had finished writing, Washington had disposed of his entire estate, conservatively valued at well over half a million dollars. His land holdings alone numbered more than 33,000 acres in states ranging from Virginia to New York to Kentucky, as well as the Northwest Territory. Stocks held in various entities, including early canal companies that he had a hand in organizing, totaled more than $25,000, while the livestock at Mount Vernon and its neighboring farms along the Potomac was valued at $15,653.

A little more than five months later, during the early morning hours of December 14, Washington awakened Martha complaining of a sore throat and difficulty breathing. She begged him to send for a servant, but he steadfastly refused. Finally, at dawn, when a maid came into the room to build a fire, he instructed her to inform Lear of his weakened condition, to send for a plantation overseer named

Rawlins who was adept at bleeding, and to notify his friend and neighbor, Dr. James Craik.

Bleeding, or bloodletting, a process believed to drain "bad humors" from the human body, was an archaic yet still accepted medical practice much in vogue in America during the mid- and late eighteenth century and consisted of making a surgical incision in a vein and allowing prescribed amounts of blood to drain into a basin. The procedure was highly regarded and recommended by Benjamin Rush of Philadelphia, the former surgeon general of the Continental Army and a signer of the Declaration of Independence.

Lear prepared "a mixture of molasses, vinegar and butter," but when Washington tried to swallow the potion "he appeared to be distressed, convulsed and almost suffocated." The overseer Rawlins soon appeared, clearly distraught at being called upon to perform such a serious procedure upon his employer. "Don't be afraid," commanded the hoarse patient, later suggesting that the incision be made even larger to allow more blood to flow. Meantime, Martha sent for a second doctor and pleaded that the bleeding be stopped. After about a pint of fluid had been drained, Washington allowed Rawlins to halt the procedure until Dr. Craik arrived.

Craik had his patient gargle a mixture of tea and vinegar, applied heated blister packs to his throat, and let more blood. "No effect was produced . . . and he [Washington] continued in the same state, unable to swallow anything," wrote the anguished doctor, who instructed servants to send for a third physician. When the other two doctors, Elisha Cullen Dick, from nearby Alexandria, and Gustavus Richard Brown, from Port Tobacco, Maryland, arrived in the midafternoon, they examined the former president, then conferred with Dr. Craik.

Craik and Brown agreed that Washington was suffering from quinsy, an acute inflammation of the tonsils that sometimes led to the formation of abscesses. Dick suggested that the illness was much more serious than mere tonsillitis; he diagnosed it as "a violent inflammation of the membranes of the throat, which it had almost closed, and which, if not immediately arrested, would result in death." While Craik and Brown wanted to continue the bleeding, Dick strongly disagreed, arguing that an immediate tracheotomy be performed to enable Washington to breathe.

The tracheotomy was not performed, however, and the patient was bled once again, further weakening him. At 4:30 p.m. Washington asked Martha to retrieve two wills from his desk. When she returned with the documents, he reviewed them and told her to keep only the latest version and to destroy the earlier one. A little later he called Lear to his side. "I find I am going," he said in a low murmur that the faithful secretary could barely hear. "My breath cannot last long. I believed from the first attack it would be fatal. Do you arrange and record all my late military letters and papers—arrange my accounts and settle my books, as you know more about them than anyone else." He asked Lear if there was anything to which he needed to attend, since there was little time left. He sat for a few moments by the fire, but was so desperate for breath that he soon returned to bed. For periods of time Lear lay beside him so that he could better turn his employer's large body and, from time to time, raise him on his pillows.

In a frail voice Washington told his physicians, "I feel myself going. I thank you for your attention. You had better not take any more trouble about me; but let me go off quietly; I cannot last long," and urged them to allow him to die "without further interruption." Two of the doctors finally excused themselves and went downstairs to await the inevitable. Craik, whose close association with the former president dated all the way back to French and Indian War days, stayed by his old friend's bedside. Washington continued to weaken.

Shortly before midnight he called Craik to his side and murmured, "My breath cannot last long." Sadly, Craik motioned to Martha that the end was near.

The large mantel clock in the dining room had just chimed eleven times when the three physicians once again assembled in Washington's bedroom and looked despairingly upon his limp body, hoping against all odds that the sixty-seven-year-old warrior would show some signs of improvement. Now, as midnight rapidly approached, they glanced solemnly at each other. There was no hope in their faces.

Martha sat nearby, attended by a few house servants and Tobias Lear. The room was cold. A mid-December snowstorm had swept down the Potomac River two days earlier and sent temperatures plummeting. Rushing about to keep the cavernous Mount Vernon as warm as possible, the servants heaped several additional blankets upon Washington's listless body, leaving nothing exposed but his face.

To Lear, he called once more and whispered, "I am just going. Have me decently buried, and do not let my body be put into the vault in less than three days after I am dead. Do you understand me?" "Yes, sir," replied Lear. "'Tis well" were the last words that the master of Mount Vernon uttered.

In a few moments, surrounded by Martha, Dr. Craik, Lear, and a few of his favorite servants, Washington felt for his feeble pulse. Before Craik could reach his bedside, the president's "hand fell from his wrist," according to Lear. Martha, sitting near the foot of the bed, caught the secretary's eye and asked, "Is he gone?" Lear nodded that it was over.

DEALING WITH HIGHWAYMEN

Mississippi, 1804

It seems that whenever the subject of outlaws is brought up, thoughts automatically travel to the post–Civil War period of the trans-Mississippi West, with its decades-long plethora of bank robberies, range wars, vigilantism, and lynchings. Few people stop to think that outlaws had ancestors, too, and that the idea of committing sins against society has been around for a very long time.

In America, some of the earliest incidents of mass lawlessness occurred not west of the mighty Mississippi River, but in the Old South, particularly in the present-day states of Mississippi, Louisiana, Tennessee, and Kentucky. Indeed, during the last quarter of the eighteenth century and the first third of the nineteenth, this huge territory was a hotbed of criminal activity that made some of the Old West's escapades look like child's play.

During the earlier years, a particularly dangerous part of the region was the section traversed by the Natchez Trace. This early thoroughfare—quite possibly the oldest road in North America—linked the town of Natchez, Mississippi, in the south, with Nashville,

Tennessee, to the north. For some 450 miles, the trail cut its way through a virgin wilderness frequented only by wild animals, Indians, and outlaws.

During the early days of Kentucky and Tennessee statehood (realized in 1792 and 1796, respectively), it was customary for farm produce raised in those states to be shipped, usually via flatboats, down one of the larger streams in the region to the Ohio River, then down the Ohio to the Mississippi, and then downstream to Natchez or New Orleans, there to be sold. At market, the farmer not only disposed of his goods, but also sold his flatboat and other equipment as well, since passage back home via river—upstream—was virtually impossible.

Prior to 1811, when the steamboat was introduced on the Mississippi River and its tributary system, thus allowing the homeward journey to be easily made by boat, the Natchez Trace provided the only cleared, overland passage between Natchez and the Tennessee and Kentucky settlements. So, after disposing of his merchandise at market, the farmer simply set out northward along the Natchez Trace, either on foot or on horseback, and eventually wound up in Nashville, where he continued to his farm. Outlaws and highwaymen soon learned that these returning farmer-merchants usually carried large sums of money derived from the sale of their farm goods and boats and that they provided "easy pickings" for those who preferred to steal what they could rather than work for a living.

Two early outlaws who preyed upon travelers along the Natchez Trace and the lower Mississippi River were Samuel Mason and Wiley Harpe. Mason was born in Virginia in 1750 and rose to the rank of captain in the American army during the Revolution. He was a highly respected soldier and accompanied General George Rogers Clark during the American attack on Vincennes in present-day Indiana. Following the war, Mason operated a tavern in Wheeling, Virginia (now West Virginia), but growing restless for excitement, he turned to a life of crime. In time, he was forced to leave his home, taking refuge in the notorious gathering place for outlaws, river pirates, and highwaymen—Cave-in-Rock, on the lower Ohio River. From there he moved to the Natchez Trace and lower Mississippi River regions, where he quickly established himself as a living legend.

Unlike Mason, with his impressive background, Wiley Harpe and his criminal brother, Micajah, were natural-born killers from their very early days and demonstrated absolutely no regard for human life. They originally operated out of East Tennessee, but created such havoc with their misdeeds that they eventually gravitated to the wilderness realm of Middle Tennessee, Kentucky, and Mississippi.

By 1802 Mississippi Territory's second governor, William C.C. Claiborne, was almost out of patience with the outlawry being committed in his region. He was a Thomas Jefferson appointee who was practicing law in Nashville when he received the job. On April 27, 1802, the twenty-seven-year-old governor sent a letter from the capital at Washington (Mississippi Territory) to the commander of a U.S. Army detachment located in the Northern end of the territory. In the epistle, Claiborne told the army officer, "I have received information that the road from this territory to Tennessee [the Natchez Trace] is infested by a daring set of robbers, among them are a certain Samuel Mason and a certain Wiley Harp[e]," adding, "I hope, Sir, that if you should receive information of any mischief being done or attempted in the wilderness you will immediately order out a party of men, and make the necessary exertions to arrest the offenders."

At some point the contents of Claiborne's letter must have become known to Mason and Harpe, who by now were on the run, supposedly somewhere in Mississippi Territory. Afraid of being apprehended by the army, the Mason gang gravitated to the area around New Madrid in Spanish Louisiana (present-day Missouri), where Mason and several of his sons were promptly arrested by Spanish authorities. Harpe was noticeably absent, but not a man by the name of John Setton, who later was revealed to actually be Harpe.

On March 26, 1803, while the arrested Mason gang was on its way to Natchez to be turned over to American officials, Samuel Mason and several others escaped, only to be seen fifteen miles northeast of Natchez on the Choctaw Trace near Cole's Creek. A militia party was dispatched to re-arrest the gang but failed, and the fleeing outlaws, now wanted by both Spanish and American authorities, scattered across the countryside, desperately seeking refuge.

By now Mason had quite a reward on his head, and it made no difference whether he was brought in dead or alive. The bounty money proved too much for Setton (actually Wiley Harpe) and another gang member named James May. The story goes that somewhere in Jefferson County, Mississippi, Harpe and May chanced upon Mason and the rest of the gang and convinced Mason that their allegiances were with him. What happened next was described by an early scholar, John W. Monette, who wrote in 1848:

> *Two of his band [supposedly Harpe and May], tempted by the large reward, concerted a plan by which they might obtain it. An opportunity soon occurred, and while Mason, in company with the two conspirators, was counting out some ill-gotten plunder, a tomahawk was buried in his brain. His head was severed from his body and borne in triumph to Washington, the seat of the territorial [Mississippi] government.*

As Harpe and May appeared before a judge to petition for their reward money, they were both arrested, based on testimony by a man who reported that they had recently robbed him and some companions on the Natchez Trace and, in so doing, had killed a fellow traveler. Meanwhile, an onlooker positively identified Setton as the notorious Wiley Harpe. The pair was transported to the Natchez jail for safekeeping, but now, with no reward money forthcoming for Mason's head and with murder and armed robbery charges hanging over them, the outlaws' only alternative was to, once again, go on the lam. Their flight from justice was cut short, however, by their capture in nearby Greeneville, Jefferson County (not to be confused with today's Greeneville in Washington County).

A grand jury sitting in Greeneville heard both men's cases on January 13, 1804. Indictments for armed robbery were rendered in both, and the men were remanded for trial. The murder charges were ignored, since conviction for armed robbery brought the death penalty anyway. On February 4 both Harpe and May were found guilty and sentenced "that on Wednesday the eighth day of the present month he be taken to the place of execution and there hung by the neck, between the hours of ten o'clock in the forenoon and four in the afternoon, until he is dead, dead, dead."

When execution day arrived, Harpe and May were taken to a place that came to be called the "Gallows Field," just outside town. A pole was horizontally suspended between the high branches of two nearby trees, and ropes were dropped from the pole. Two ladders were rested upon the pole, and the men were forced to climb the ladders. Each man's hands and feet were bound and a noose placed around his neck. When the ladders were kicked from beneath the men, they became suspended in space, hanging there until death took its toll.

One early authority, Franklin L. Riley, writing in 1902, declared that after the hanging of the two outlaws, "their heads were placed on poles, one a short distance to the north and the other a short distance to the west of Green[e]ville, on the Natchez Trace." Legend has it that the men's bodies were buried nearby.

SHAKERTOWN,
VILLAGE OF YESTERYEAR

Kentucky, 1806

Situated along the palisades of the Kentucky River, a northward-flowing tributary of the Ohio, is the quaint little village of Pleasant Hill. Encompassing several hundred acres of Kentucky's finest bluegrass region, Pleasant Hill was once the seat of the second most important Shaker colony in the United States. At its height the religious settlement, characterized by its unique architecture, claimed some five hundred inhabitants and three thousand acres of the best farmland in Kentucky.

But the epic of Shakertown, as the village eventually became known to its neighbors, includes more than just stories about productive farmland and quaint houses. It is a complex narrative that begins with the origin of the Shaker religion in England during the mid-1700s, and follows the village's life and times to its final demise and the extinction of the Shaker religion in Kentucky in the early part of twentieth century. It is the tale of a strange religion, dominated by a woman believed to be the spiritual daughter of God. And finally, it is the account of an industrious people who, because of their many contributions to society as a whole, have made the world a better place in which to live.

It all began in England in 1747 when a Manchester-born Quaker woman named Ann Lee expressed radical ideas foreign to the Quaker philosophy. Lee was subsequently expelled from the Quaker Church, and it was the sudden awakening that she underwent during this critical period in her religious experience that provided the background for the birth and growth of the Shaker faith.

During her ostracism, the tenets of the Shaker religion were formulated in Lee's mind. Although the records are sketchy regarding her activities immediately after her conversion, they do show that she and some followers emigrated to New York in 1774. Within two years of her arrival in America, Mother Ann, as she was now known, established a Shaker settlement at Watervlet, New York. During the next several years, she extended her dominion throughout a large portion of the northeastern United States. By 1843 Shaker influence had spread so rapidly that at least nineteen permanent colonies were scattered across Maine, New York, Massachusetts, Connecticut, New Hampshire, Ohio, Indiana, and Kentucky.

The colony at Pleasant Hill, Kentucky, dates back to 1806, when a few members from a newly formed colony at Union Village, Ohio, left for unexplored territory and settled at Elisha Tomas's farm, Shawnee Run, along the Kentucky River. The number of migrants was so large and the size of the temporary home grew to such proportions that soon a new site had to be found. By 1812 Pleasant Hill was established, rapidly becoming the most important Shaker colony in the United States, outside of New Lebanon, New York. Land at the new site was acquired gradually—either through gift or purchase—until Shakertown could point with pride to the fact that more than three thousand acres of surrounding countryside fell within its ownership.

This vast quantity of land and its quality coincided well with the basic beliefs and doctrines of the Shakers. An agricultural people, they believed that hard work stood second only to their religion—and hard work they performed when it came to farming. Half of Shakertown's total acreage was devoted to the raising of such crops as oats, corn, potatoes, wheat, broom corn, and hay, in addition to such fruits as apples, peaches, pears, strawberries, and raspberries. Though all of the colony's residents assisted in the annual harvest of these crops, it was sometimes necessary to hire up to sixty outside hands, at about two dollars a day each, to get the harvest in on time.

The Shakers produced all of their own butter, cheese, and preserves, becoming some of the first people to actually utilize cans for preserving vegetables. They originated the idea of using dried sweet corn for food, and became the first people anywhere to offer food seed in packets for future plantings.

The Shakers' main role in life, however, was to dedicate themselves to their religion. In addition to the supreme belief that Mother Ann was the spiritual daughter of God, Shakers were also convinced that marriage was not a Christian institution. They, therefore, insisted on a life of celibacy for each and every member of the society. The colony was propagated by assimilating families who already had children, or by allowing orphans and runaway children to become a part of the village. They believed that God was both male and female, and that angels and spirits also possessed gender. A belief in community ownership of property is obvious from the vast agricultural holdings that the colony possessed and the communal dwellings and work areas apparent in the village. A dancing ritual in which participants sometimes experienced violent shaking is responsible for the name that was eventually bestowed upon them.

Shakers differed from most of today's Christian denominations. They completely eliminated the Lord's Supper and water baptism from their services, and they believed in their own power over physical diseases. They saw visions, possessed the gift of prophecy, and put great stock in spiritual dreams. Last but not least, Shakers believed in a strong detachment from the rest of the world.

Shaker government consisted of elders and elderesses who "had charge of the spiritual welfare of society and exercised a general supervision over the doings of lesser officials," along with deacons and deaconesses who were "entrusted with the temporal affairs of the activity to which they were assigned." Two trustees, one male and one female, dealt with the outside community in fiscal matters and other public-related affairs.

At its height, Shakertown consisted of about twenty buildings. For purposes of administrative control, the village was divided into several sections. The smaller units consisted of the Center, the East, the West, and the North Families and the West Lot. Each of the families was controlled by an elder and elderess, along with a deacon and deaconess. Each family had its family dwelling, which was a large residence with workrooms, bedrooms, kitchen, dining area, and assembly hall. Entry to the family dwellings was by one of two doors, the left one for males and the right one for females. Although both doors opened into a common hallway, two separate sets of stairs, one for the men and one for the women, reached to the top floors.

Industry and handicraft played a great part in the lives of the Shaker people. In pursuing their day-to-day existence, the Shakers invented some devices that have since become universal in use and acceptance. The first buzz saw used in the United States is attributed to Shakertown. The Shakers made famous the so-called broad, or Shaker, broom. They invented and frequently used a four-wheeled wagon that could be rocked back on two wheels and dumped like a cart.

Shakers maintained their own sawmills and were noted for their furniture-making abilities. They ground their own meal and spun their own cloth. In addition, they built and maintained the first automated waterworks west of the Appalachian Mountains. From a cistern, water was pumped by horsepower through lead pipes to the village. All of this was accomplished sixty years before nearby Harrodsburg had a water system of its own.

Shakertown began to decline after the Civil War. The great conflict had placed tremendous strains on the society, and both factions, Union and Confederate, had often helped themselves to the hospitality of the kind people. Converts became more difficult to obtain to replace the dying members, and with the arrival of no children except for orphans, it was difficult to keep the fires of religious zeal burning. The village's surrounding land was eventually traded to a local man in return for the promise of perpetual upkeep for the remaining members of the sect. The official dissolution occurred in 1910.

THE CAPTURE OF AARON BURR

Mississippi, 1807

Aaron Burr was a wanted man. For several months he had stayed one step ahead of federal authorities who were trying to arrest him on charges of conspiring against the United States government. The former vice president in Thomas Jefferson's first administration (1801–5) had been accused of masterminding a plot to separate from the Union the Old Southwest, and joining with it in organizing a new government with strong allegiances with Spain.

Rumors had flown in Washington, the small capital of Mississippi Territory located six miles up the Natchez Trace from Natchez, that Burr and a flotilla of soldiers and weapons were descending the Mississippi River and would soon be in the vicinity. On December 20, 1806, anxious residents of Washington gathered to read President Jefferson's recent proclamation on the matter, although Burr was not mentioned by name, nor was his intention to separate the western states and territories from the Union. "Information has been received that sundry persons—are conspiring and confederating together to begin—a military expedition or enterprise against the dominions of

Spain," the document read, and issued a "warning . . . enjoining all faithful citizens who have been led without due knowledge or consideration to participate in the said unlawful enterprise to withdraw from the same without delay."

The citizens of Washington, however, as well as residents throughout the country, already knew the real purpose of Burr's enterprise, as evidenced by a journal entry made by U.S. Senator William Plumer one day after the president's proclamation:

> *Reports have for some time circulated from one end of the United States to the other, that Aaron Burr—with others, in the western States are preparing gun boats, provisions, money, men, &c to make war upon the Spaniards in South America—that his intention is to establish a new empire in the western world & That he contemplates forming this Empire from South America & the western States of North America.*

As expected, Burr soon arrived in Mississippi, but he crossed the river to the Louisiana side. Learning of his imminent arrest, he surrendered to the acting governor of Mississippi Territory on January 17, 1807, denying all the time participating in the nefarious scheme of which he was accused. He was taken back across the Mississippi River to nearby Washington, where the following month he was examined by the grand jury, which ruled that insufficient evidence precluded it from charging him with treason. Burr was released, but his supposed innocence notwithstanding, he was ordered to remain in the territorial capital. Instead, he fled the area the following day, and now local officials found themselves looking for him in the backwoods of southern Mississippi.

Following his illegal flight from Washington, Burr headed toward Fort Stoddert, a small army post near the Tombigbee River in present-day Alabama and about 175 miles east of the territorial capital. What he did or where he went for the next two weeks is unknown. However, at around eleven o'clock on the night of February 18, 1807, he and a fellow conspirator, Chester (some authorities say Robert) Ashley, approached the courthouse at Wakefield, the county seat of Washington County, Mississippi Territory (now Alabama). As their horses sloshed through the muddy street, the pair spotted a man near the building and turned toward him. He was Nicholas Perkins, a local attorney and the registrar of the land office.

Perkins was asked the directions to Major James Hinson's house, where the two men told him they would spend the night. Perkins told them Hinson lived about seven or eight miles from town, along a horribly maintained road, and that the bridge might be washed out from the recent torrential rains. Nevertheless, the two said they would proceed. As they rode away, Perkins noticed that one of the men sported a splendid pair of riding boots, but otherwise had gone to some lengths to disguise himself as an ordinary farmer.

The suspicious lawyer awakened the sheriff, told him he thought that one of the two riders was the fugitive Aaron Burr, and persuaded the lawman to accompany him out to Major Hinson's farm. When they arrived, Mrs. Hinson was preparing food for the two strangers. Perkins got a good look at the pair, then excused himself, saying that he was returning to the courthouse. The sheriff stayed behind with the Hinsons.

Perkins, rather than go back to town, rode the wind to Fort Stoddert, several miles away, and reported his suspicions to the post's commandant, Lieutenant Edmund Pendleton Gaines. Gaines, Perkins, and a contingent of soldiers returned to the Hinson farm, but along the way, encountered Burr headed toward freedom. He was placed under arrest for the second time and returned to Fort Stoddert, where his charming manner impressed everyone, including Mrs. Gaines, with whom he played chess.

It appeared to Gaines that affairs over the "Burr Conspiracy" were coming to a rapid head, so rather than wait for orders from his superiors, he entrusted his prisoner to Perkins with instructions to accompany him to Washington, D.C. "It strikes me as an indispensable step for the security of this settlement and the tranquility of the Western Country generally, to send the Col. to Washington City and leave this place at all events by the 22nd of the present month. . . . I apprehend that something is brewing below, and I must secure this place," he wrote.

Burr was not alone in his bold undertaking of trying to establish a new nation from the western states of the Union. His number two man in the scheme was General James Wilkinson, the governor of Louisiana Territory and ranking member of the U.S. Army. Within the last few years, Wilkinson had become Burr's close friend and confidant, and when the former vice president championed a course of destiny for the new western states and territories, Wilkinson became a willing disciple.

Wilkinson, with his two high-ranking government posts, was in a perfect position to further Burr's plans. In midsummer 1806 he dispatched a young army lieutenant, Zebulon M. Pike, on a combination exploring and spying mission to the distant Southwest, that region still owned by Spain and encompassing much of present-day Texas, New Mexico, Arizona, and Colorado. Pike was to not only learn the lay of the land and collect data about the various Indian tribes, flora, and fauna, but at the same time he was ordered to gather intelligence about the "settlements of New Mexico" in the event information of this nature might be needed in furthering Burr's scheme.

On June 11, 1806, even before Pike and his small command began preparations for their long journey to the Southwest, Wilkinson had received orders from Secretary of War Henry Dearborn, instructing him to proceed to the lower Mississippi River valley to fortify the army command in the South for a possible conflict with Spain. A short time after reaching his new headquarters at Natchitoches, Wilkinson received a disturbing letter from Aaron Burr, its contents revealing that the former vice president was ready to put his filibustering scheme into action. He told Wilkinson that he would be in Natchez in mid-December in order to meet with him and discuss plans.

When he finished reading the letter, Wilkinson began to brood. This was not the time to be plotting against the United States government, he thought. He considered the frightening situation in which he found himself and wondered how he might escape from it unscathed. The facts as he saw them if he continued his participation in Burr's scheme were obvious: he might be arrested and lose his positions as commanding general of the army and territorial governor; Burr's scheme for creating a separate empire in the Southwest had been exposed on the front page of practically every newspaper in the country, and American citizens in the East were howling for his blood; and he, Wilkinson, still had not heard from Lieutenant Pike about what was going on in New Mexico. Clearly, if Wilkinson was ever going to make an effort to salvage his career, now was the time. He must distance himself from Burr and his cohorts.

It took Wilkinson a little more than a week after the receipt of Burr's letter to decide what he must do to get back in the good graces of President Jefferson and other officials in Washington. He wrote the president a personal letter in which he described "in a dramatic, even hysterical, manner," according to one of his biographers, his "discovery" of a serious plot under way to destroy the integrity of the United States. Having learned of the situation, he wrote, he was prepared to patch up the peace with the Spaniards in Texas and to devote his full energies to this sinister conspiracy. Since "a numerous and powerful association, extending from New York through the western states to the territories bordering on the Mississippi, has been formed with the design to levy and rendezvous eight or ten thousand men in New Orleans," he declared that he would proceed to the city at once to defend it from the filibusterers. Jefferson swallowed Wilkinson's lies hook, line, and sinker and issued what would today be called an "all points bulletin" for the arrest of Aaron Burr, a move that eventually led to the former vice president's arrest in Washington, Mississippi Territory, and his subsequent capture in Wakefield.

Perkins departed Fort Stoddert for Washington, D.C., with his prisoner on March 5, 1807, and had successfully transported him as far as Fredericksburg, Virginia, when a messenger from the capital intercepted them and directed them to proceed instead to Richmond, where the trial was to be held. On June 24 a grand jury indicted Burr on both treason and misdemeanor charges after hearing testimony from his one time associate, General Wilkinson. The trial began on August 3, with Chief Justice of the U.S. Supreme Court John Marshall presiding. After nearly a month of testimony, Justice Marshall read his three-hour-long instructions to the jury on August 31, and admonished jury members to "apply that law to the facts, and . . . find a verdict of guilty or not guilty as their own consciences may direct." Within twenty-five minutes the jury foreman declared, "We of the jury say that Aaron Burr is not proved to be guilty under this indictment by any evidence submitted to us," adding, "We therefore find him not guilty."

Wilkinson served several more years in the army and was honorably discharged in 1815. He died as a land speculator in Mexico in 1825, carrying his secrets to an unmarked grave in Mexico City. Burr died, tired and impoverished, in 1836.

MERIWETHER LEWIS'S
LAST JOURNEY

Tennessee, 1809

When Meriwether Lewis left Saint Louis in late summer 1809 on a trip to the nation's capital, Tennessee was the furthest thing from his mind. But Lewis never arrived in Washington, and his violent death on the Natchez Trace remains a mystery to this day.

Soon after Lewis and his partner, William Clark, returned to Saint Louis in 1806, fresh from their monumental exploration of the American West, Lewis was appointed governor of that vast territory known as Louisiana by his friend and confidant, President Thomas Jefferson. With headquarters in Saint Louis, Lewis pursued his duties as chief executive of the region for more than a year, when, in mid-1809, he decided to journey to Washington to straighten out some territorial finances. While in the East, he also intended to follow up on the publication of the journals he and Clark kept during their almost two-and-a-half-year, eight-thousand-mile trip to the Pacific Ocean and back.

Lewis's original plans called for him to travel down the Mississippi River from Saint Louis to New Orleans, then to sail around

Florida and up the Atlantic coast to Washington. However, when he arrived at Chickasaw Bluffs, the site of present-day Memphis, he decided instead to march eastward, cross-country to the Natchez Trace, and follow the wilderness road northward to Nashville, then to Knoxville, and finally to the capital.

On the evening of October 10, 1809, the travel-weary explorer approached Grinder's Stand, a small hostelry located on the Trace some sixty miles south of Nashville. As he neared the log building, situated in a clearing in the otherwise thick forest, he met Mrs. Robert Grinder, the wife of the owner, who was away at the time. With Lewis was his servant, Pernia, and a slave belonging to Major James Neelly, the agent for the Chickasaw nation. Neelly was to catch up later.

Lewis asked Mrs. Grinder for accommodations. Later in the evening, after he had finished dining, he retired to a tiny room designated for him by his hostess. During the night Mrs. Grinder was awakened by gunshots and, believing that they came from Lewis's room, cracked his door open to peek in. Horrified, she found her guest conscious, but with two gaping wounds, one in the head and the other in the chest. When he saw Mrs. Grinder, Lewis cried, "Dear madam, be so good as to give me a little water." But rather than retrieve water for the wounded man, the terrified woman refused to enter the room until the sun came up. When she finally approached Lewis again, he said, "Dear madam, look at my wounds." When Mrs. Grinder asked him how he was injured, he gave a strange reply: "If I had not done it somebody else would." He then exclaimed, "Oh how hard it is to die, I am so strong!" Within minutes, America's best-known explored was dead and one of the nation's longest-running unsolved mysteries was born. Lewis was interred near the Grinder house, where, years later, a stone monument marking the burial site was erected by the state of Tennessee.

From Nashville, on October 18, 1809, Lewis's traveling companion, Major Neelly, wrote to Thomas Jefferson, "It is with extreme pain that I have to inform you of the death of His Excellency Meriwether Lewis, Governor of upper Louisiana who died the morning of the 11th Instant and I am sorry to say by Suicide."

Immediately after Lewis's death, the question arose whether he had committed suicide or was the victim of foul play, a common occurrence in those days on the outlaw-infested Natchez Trace. Thomas Jefferson, who probably knew Lewis as well as anyone else, assumed that his friend had taken his own life. In the introduction to the journals of the expedition to the Pacific, which were finally published in 1814, Jefferson wrote:

> *Governor Lewis had, from early life, been subject to hypochondriac afflictions. It was a constitutional disposition in all of the nearer branches of the family of his name, and was more immediately inherited by him from his father.*

Of the actual event, Jefferson wrote, "About three o'clock in the night he did the deed which plunged his friends into affliction, and deprived his country of one of her most valued citizens." Yet, if Jefferson knew that Lewis was as hypochondria-prone as he indicated, why would he have entrusted him with the command of the most important western exploration in the history of the country?

The possibility of Lewis being afflicted with some kind of illness that could have resulted in suicide was reflected in his personal correspondence of the time. Although he confided in a letter to a friend in August before departing Saint Louis that "I shall leave the Territory in the most perfect state of Tranquility," when he arrived at

Chickasaw Bluffs in September, he wrote to President James Madison that he was "much exhausted from the heat of the climate," but that after medicating himself, he felt much better. During his stay at Chickasaw Bluffs, Lewis also wrote to Major Amos Stoddard, the commandant at nearby Fort Pickering, that "my indisposition has induced me to change my rout [to Washington]."

Lewis's health is also an issue addressed in remarks made by contemporaries upon learning of his death. The eminent Philadelphia artist Charles Willson Peale wrote to his son, Rembrandt, in November 1809, declaring that "Governor Lewis has destroyed himself," adding, "It is said that he had been sometime past in bad health & showed evident signs of disarrangement."

Suicide or murder? To this day, no one knows for sure. Despite modern tests by forensic scientists from George Washington University, the truth of the matter is that unless the body of Meriwether Lewis is exhumed and scientifically examined, it will never be known whether this icon of American history lost his life on Middle Tennessee's Natchez Trace from his own hand or if he was brutally murdered by suspects unknown.

MAYHEM ON THE KENTUCKY FRONTIER

Kentucky, 1811

It was a macabre sight that presented itself to all of the frightened slaves assembled inside the small, one-room, log kitchen cabin that sat in the Kentucky woods near the Ohio River. At the command of their master, Lilburne Lewis—gentleman farmer, affluent member of Livingston County society, and a nephew of former president Thomas Jefferson—several of the servants had been ordered to leave their own living cabins during the late evening of Sunday, December 15, 1811, and to gather in the kitchen, situated just a short distance from Lewis's main house at Rocky Hill Plantation. When the slaves entered the cabin, they discovered that the only other white man present was Lilburne's younger brother, Isham. They became concerned when they quickly sensed that both of the Lewis brothers were drunk, since Lilburne especially had been known to abuse his servants during his drinking bouts.

Lilburne soon made the small crowd of slaves aware of why they had been called out into the night. Stretched out before him, tightly bound with rope and secured to the rough, puncheon floor, was seventeen-year-old George, one of Lilburne's house servants whom contemporaries described as "ill-grown [and] ill-thrived." Lilburne, expressing displeasure over the fact that George had recently dropped and broken a valuable water pitcher, told his terrified audience that he intended to teach one and all a lesson in submission. As he ordered several of the slaves to build a roaring blaze in the kitchen's huge fireplace, Lilburne retrieved an ax from the corner of the cabin, strolled over to the door and locked it, and then approached the horrified George, who by now must have foreseen that his master meant to kill him.

While Isham and the distressed slaves watched, Lilburne lifted the ax above his head and brought it down upon George's neck with a resounding thud. The blow nearly decapitated George and left a gaping three-inch-deep gash in his throat. Within seconds, the slave's lifeblood drained from the wound as he lay silent upon the floor.

With Isham's help, Lilburne then wrestled with one of the more powerfully built slaves, forced the bloody ax into the frightened man's hands, and demanded that he dismember George's dead body. When the gruesome deed was done, the pieces of poor George's corpse were thrown into the blazing fireplace, while Lilburne warned his slaves to keep silent about the incident they had just witnessed lest they receive the same treatment.

Midnight slipped by during the sickening proceedings, and at around two o'clock on Monday morning, the region for miles around was shaken by the first shock of the now-famous New Madrid earthquake. While Lilburne, Isham, and the dumbfounded slaves watched, the entire kitchen fireplace crumbled before their eyes and quickly extinguished the flames, consequently ending the fiery demise of George's slowly burning body. Helpless to do anything else until daylight, Lilburne ordered the slaves back to their quarters with a repeated warning to keep quiet.

When Lilburne himself returned to his own home, his wife was waiting for him. According to a description of the incident, written by Lewis's preacher, she exclaimed, "O! Mr. Lewis, where have you been and what have you done!" Continuing, the minister wrote:

She had heard a strange pounding, and dreadful screams, and had smelled something like fresh meat burning! He said that he had never enjoyed himself at a ball so well as he had enjoyed himself that evening.

Shortly after daybreak, Lilburne ordered several slaves to rebuild the destroyed kitchen fireplace and chimney. As the earthquake's tremors continued to rock the surrounding countryside all day, Lilburne pulled pieces of George's partially burned body out of the debris and attempted to hide them in the slowly rising rockwork. Content that George's remains had been properly concealed, the unrepentant Lilburne went about his way, no doubt self-assured that his deed would never be discovered. And, he must have thought, what if his secret was found out? Nothing would come of it since, under Kentucky law, slaves could not testify against their masters, and his own brother, Isham, was the only other eyewitness to the crime.

But Lilburne had a powerful, unknown enemy: the recurring series of earthquakes that continued to pound the countryside day after day, week after week. Sometime in late January or early February 1812, a particularly strong tremor once again demolished the kitchen chimney and fireplace, and when the masonry came rolling down, George's partially decomposed head came tumbling down with it. A stray dog found the head and was investigating it when he was spotted by a neighbor, who took the remains to the sheriff.

It didn't take long for the authorities' suspicions to become aroused. No one remembered seeing George for a long time, and now his head mysteriously rolls out of Lilburne Lewis's kitchen chimney. Quick investigative work by the sheriff built a solid case against the Lewis brothers, and in March evidence substantiating their involvement in the slave's murder was presented to a grand jury, which quickly returned an indictment against Lilburne, but not Isham. A second grand jury was summoned the following day, at which time true bills were returned on both brothers. In the quaint writing style of the day, the indictments read:

> . . . *said Lilbourn [sic] Lewis senior with a certain ax there & then had & held in both his hands . . . did strike cut and penetrate in & upon the neck of him the said Negro Boy George giving to the said Negro Boy, George . . . one Mortal wound of the Breadth of four inches and of the Depth of three inches of which said mortal wound he . . . Instantly did die in the county of Livingston . . . and that . . . Isham Lewis then & there feloniously wilfully Violently and of his malice aforethought was present aiding helping abetting comforting assisting and maintaining the said Lilbourn Lewis senior.*

Between the time that the Lewis brothers' indictments were returned in mid-March 1812 and the time set for the murder trial the following June, the men were free on bond. Lilburne, with the strong sense that he would either be hanged for George's killing or incarcerated for a long period of time, discussed his miserable situation with Isham, and the two decided to commit suicide. Following a carefully thought-out plan, the brothers went to the local cemetery on April 10, each armed with a flintlock rifle. The scheme was simple: The brothers would stand a few yards apart on each side of the small cemetery and, upon a given signal, simultaneously fire at the chest of the other. In the event one of the rifles misfired, Lilburne explained, the survivor would correct the situation by propping the re-primed weapon upon the ground with the muzzle pointing toward the heart, and then releasing the trigger using a length of tree branch. As Lilburne demonstrated how simple the procedure would be, he accidentally tripped the rifle's trigger and the ball went smashing through his heart. He died instantly.

The incredulous Isham, now completely terrified and disenchanted with the entire suicide idea, quickly fled the cemetery. During the coroner's inquest into Lilburne's death, the younger brother was found to be an accessory to the murder. He was arrested, then released, arrested again, and held for not only being an accomplice in George's murder, but in Lilburne's suicide as well.

On May 5, several weeks before his case was to go to trial, Isham escaped from jail and headed for parts unknown. He was never seen in Livingston County, Kentucky, again.

GUNFIGHT ON NASHVILLE'S PUBLIC SQUARE

Tennessee, 1813

Perhaps no two men were more influential in shaping American history and molding the nation's destiny during the first half of the nineteenth century than Nashvillian Andrew Jackson and neighboring Williamson County resident Thomas Hart Benton. The close personal relationship of these two political giants during their tenure in the federal government is widely known. Jackson, as president of the United States, and Benton, as U.S. senator from Missouri and the leading advocate for the nation's rapid expansion all the way to the Pacific Ocean, were towering figures in the 1820s and 1830s who, either personally or through the control they held over others, dominated national politics for many years.

What is not so widely known, however, is the fact that the two men were not always on such friendly terms. A gunfight on the Public Square in Nashville in 1813 temporarily halted a warm friendship that had been building for several years. The fracas left a ball in Jackson's arm which plagued him for two decades, while for Benton it meant ostracism from the Middle Tennessee community where Jackson's popularity was riding an all-time high.

To understand the conflict that took place on that long-ago day and to draw any intelligent conclusions from it, one must appreciate the high moral code prevalent on the frontier, and further, understand the positions that honor and principle played in the lives of both Jackson and Benton. Having been raised in like environments and pursuing similar lifestyles as young men, the confrontation was unavoidable when measured against the ethical standards of the day and the close resemblance between the personalities of the two men.

Andrew Jackson had moved to Nashville in 1788. Born in South Carolina in 1767 of modest parentage, he had traveled to Tennessee (then part of North Carolina) in pursuit of a legal career. In Nashville, he fell in love with the daughter of the town's co-founder, John Donelson. Taking Rachel Donelson as his wife, he built his home east of town and began a life of respect and relative prosperity. A rapid succession of public offices—attorney general for the Western District of North Carolina upon his arrival in Nashville; Tennessee's first U.S. representative in 1796, when statehood was attained; U.S. senator in 1797; justice of the Tennessee supreme court in 1798; and major-general of the Tennessee militia in 1802—had earned Jackson an almost godlike veneration from the populace of his adopted state.

Thomas Hart Benton was born near Hillsboro, North Carolina, in 1782, the son of Jesse Benton, a well-known land speculator. Jesse died when Tom was only eight years old, leaving his wife, eight children, and several thousand acres of land across the Appalachian Mountains near Nashville. When Tom was about nineteen years old, the widow Benton with all of her children and slaves moved to Williamson County, Tennessee. There they began farming the estate left by the elder Benton, and young Tom eventually became a lawyer, practicing his craft in Franklin, the county seat. He served in the Tennessee senate from 1809 to 1811 and joined the Tennessee militia, which was commanded by Andrew Jackson at the time, where he was quickly promoted to colonel.

In October 1812, four months after the declaration of war with Great Britain, the U.S. War Department requested 1,500 soldiers from Tennessee to support General James Wilkinson, the commandant at New Orleans. Governor Willie Blount instructed Jackson to raise the troops and to assume their command. By early December, Jackson had mobilized more than two thousand men, assembled them in Nashville, and prepared them for the journey to New Orleans.

One of Jackson's right-hand men was Benton, who commanded a regiment of infantry. The troops moved out of Nashville in January 1813. Jackson and two infantry regiments, including the one commanded by Benton, traveled by water down the Cumberland, Ohio, and Mississippi Rivers. When the army arrived in Natchez on February 15, Jackson found that his command had been "dismissed from public service." The orders left Jackson in somewhat of a dilemma—he was 450 miles from home with more than two thousand soldiers and no war to fight.

Jackson steadfastly refused to dismiss his troops to get back on their own to Tennessee, preferring to march them back himself. In so doing, however, he amassed a sizable personal debt for their food, supplies, and transportation. When the army finally returned to Nashville, Benton decided to go to Washington to seek a commission in the regular army. While in the nation's capital, he volunteered to seek redress from the War Department for the $12,000 that Jackson had advanced to the war effort. Benton was successful in both of his missions and started back home to Nashville.

In the meantime, Benton's brother Jesse had involved himself in a personal disagreement between William Carroll, a close friend of Andrew Jackson and his brigade inspector, and Littleton Johnston, a recently mustered-out lieutenant in the now-defunct volunteer army. Carroll refused to duel Johnston, but when he was challenged by Johnston's friend, Jesse Benton, he accepted. Carroll immediately went to Jackson and asked him to serve as his second in the upcoming duel. Jackson was hesitant to involve himself in what he considered to be a private matter, but after much cajoling by Carroll, he finally agreed. The duel was held, both men were slightly wounded, tempers waned, and all was well, at least for the time being.

Thomas Benton was en route to Nashville from Washington when he received the news about Jackson standing in as a second in a duel against his brother. Having just been Jackson's spokesman at the War Department and having satisfactorily resolved his mentor's financial problems, Tom was furious to learn that Jackson would even consider participating in the duel and, upon his arrival in Nashville, he made it known that he was not happy with his former commander's involvement.

The entire affair might have blown over uneventfully had Jackson's political enemies not seen fit to keep the flames of anger burning between the two men. Finally, when the claims and counterclaims became so distorted that Jackson's compulsive temper got the upper hand, he threatened to publicly horsewhip Tom Benton. His chance to fulfill the promise came on September 4, 1813, when Nashville awoke to find both Benton brothers and the general in town at the same time.

Jackson—along with Colonel John Coffee, an associate during the Natchez expedition, and Stockley Hays, Mrs. Jackson's nephew—checked in at the Nashville Inn, while the Benton brothers put up at the City Hotel across the Public Square. The confrontation came when Jackson and Coffee, as they returned from the post office, literally ran into Tom Benton, who was standing in the doorway of the City Hotel. Jackson approached Benton with horsewhip and pistol drawn. Backing Benton down a long hallway in the hotel, he failed to see brother Jesse taking aim with two pistols from behind. Jesse fired, both shots hitting Jackson.

Jackson fired his pistol while falling, but the ball failed to make contact with Tom, who then drew his pistols and fired, both shots missing. Coffee fired at Tom, but missed. Grasping his empty pistol as a club, he lunged toward Tom, who stepped backward and fell down a flight of stairs. Stockley Hays, meanwhile, tried to run Jesse through with a sword cane, but was foiled when the blade broke on a button. Jesse, his pistols now reloaded, tried to shoot Hays, but his weapons misfired.

Jackson was seriously injured in the tragicomic episode. The shot from one of Jesse's pistols broke his left shoulder blade, while the other discharge lodged a ball in his upper left arm. He nearly died before the blood could be stopped and, at one time, it was doubtful whether or not the doctors could save his arm. Jackson went home to the Hermitage, his estate outside Nashville, and there made a slow and painful recovery. The ball in his arm caused Jackson continuous anguish until 1832 when, as president of the United States, he finally had it removed.

After the affray, the Benton brothers left the Nashville area, never to return. Tom claimed, "I'm literally in hell here," and moved to Missouri, where a few years later he gained fame as the state's first U.S. senator, a position he held for thirty years. Jackson and Benton didn't see each other again until 1823, when both were serving in the senate in Washington. Their differences were patched up and they remained good friends and staunch political allies until Jackson's death years later. Jesse, who left for Louisiana after the fight, never forgave Jackson, nor did he condone his brother for his later support of him. As late as the presidential campaign of 1828, Jesse was still trying to discredit Andrew Jackson.

INDIAN WARFARE IN ALABAMA

Alabama, 1813-14

During the War of 1812, driven by his own hatred of Americans and prodded by Great Britain, the noted Shawnee warrior Tecumseh and his brother, the Prophet, traveled over much of the eastern United States in a last-ditch attempt to turn various Indian tribes against the federal government. Tecumseh's mission carried him deep into the South, where some of his most avid listeners were leading members of the Creek tribe, natives of Alabama.

One of the consequences of Tecumseh's visits to the Creeks was the August 30, 1813, attack on Fort Mims, located in present-day Alabama about forty miles north of Mobile, but then a part of Mississippi Territory. The assault on the fort was preceded by a confrontation a month earlier between whites and a party of Red Sticks, the warring faction of the Creeks, so called because they painted their war clubs brilliant red. In the ensuing melee, the Creeks lost a large amount of valuable powder and shot recently obtained in Florida from the Spanish. Following the fight, the whites retired to Fort Mims, a stockaded post built around Samuel Mims's house.

At around noon on the day of the attack, the Creek chief, William Weatherford, son of a white trader and a Creek woman, and about 800 warriors swept down on the structure and its garrison of some 500 to 600 white soldiers, settlers, and friendly Indians, killing about 250 and taking many more prisoner. The slaughter was horrific, one witness bemoaning "the fearful shrieks of women and children put to death in ways as horrible as Indian barbarity could invent." Scalping of the victims was rampant as the Creeks totally subdued the doomed fort. What Weatherford and his warriors failed to realize at the time, however, was that they had signed their own death warrants with their wanton murder and brutalization of the American outpost.

News of the Fort Mims massacre did not reach Nashville and Andrew Jackson, major-general of the Tennessee militia, until September 18. One week later, Tennessee governor Willie Blount was authorized to raise 3,500 Tennessee volunteers for field duty in Mississippi Territory. Jackson, still recovering from wounds suffered during his recent gunfight with the Benton brothers on Nashville's Public Square, was ordered to command the volunteer army, and by early October had assembled the complete division in Huntsville in present-day Alabama.

Jackson's army had little time to wait before they saw action with the Creeks. On November 3 General John Coffee dispatched his mounted riflemen to the Indian village of Tallushatchee, situated between two tributaries of the Coosa River near the Georgia state boundary line. In a fight that lasted only a few minutes, the village's inhabitants were thoroughly routed by Coffee's men. David (Davy) Crockett, who in later years would display heroism at the Alamo fighting for Texas independence, was a young man at the time and present at the battle. His description of the slaughter of the Creeks is disturbing, but in line with the Indian massacre at Fort Mims. Years later, in his autobiography, Crockett wrote of the incident:

> *We passed on each side of the town, keeping near to it, until our lines met on the far side. We then closed up at both ends, so as to surround it completely; and then we sent Captain Hammond's company of rangers to bring on the affray. . . . The main army was now formed in a hollow square around the town, and they pursued Hammond till they came in reach of us. We then gave them a fire, and they returned it, and then ran back into their town. We began to close on the town by making our files closer and closer, and the Indians soon saw they were our property. So most of them wanted us to take them prisoner; and their squaws and all would run and take hold of any of us they could, and give themselves up. . . . I saw some warriors run into a house, until I counted forty-six of them. We pursued them until we got near the house, when we saw a squaw sitting in the door, and she placed her feet against the bow she had in her hand, and then took an arrow, and raising her feet, she drew with all her might, and let fly at us, and she killed a man. . . . He was a lieutenant and his death so enraged us all, that she was fired on, and had at least twenty balls blown through her. This was the first man I ever saw killed with a bow and arrow. We now shot them like dogs, and then set the house on fire, and*

burned it up with the forty-six warriors in it. I recol-
lect seeing a boy who was shot down near the house.
His arm and thigh was broken, and he was so near the
burning that the grease was stewing out of him.

At Talladega on November 9, Jackson and Coffee surrounded a Creek army of seven hundred warriors. The Tennessee sharpshooters proved too much for the poorly equipped Indians, many of whom were still fighting with bows and arrows. In less than thirty minutes, the Americans had beaten the Creeks into retreat, after about five hundred of them were slain, to only fifteen of Jackson's men killed. The strength of the Creeks was not greatly diminished, however, and in three subsequent battles—at Emuckfau on January 22, 1814; at Enotachopco on January 24; and at Calibee Creek on January 27—the Indians repulsed Jackson's volunteer army.

Finally, for the Americans, the coup de grâce came on March 27, at a peninsula of land formed by the Tallapoosa River called Horseshoe Bend. There Jackson's volunteer militia, supported by artillery and assisted by another volunteer force from East Tennessee and a large contingent of Cherokee allies, decisively defeated the Creeks with a kill ratio of eight to nine hundred Indians lost compared to forty-nine of Jackson's men. The Creek leader, Weatherford, secretly visited Jackson's camp, found the general, and sued for peace. Following a long talk, Jackson released Weatherford, who promised to return to his people and demand that they lay down their arms. "I have not surrendered myself thoughtlessly," Weatherford declared. "Whilst there were chances of success I never left my post nor supplicated peace, but my people are gone, and I now ask it for my nation and for myself." Jackson was impressed with the man, who continued, "On the miseries and misfortunes brought upon my country I look back with deepest sorrow, and wish to avert still greater calamities."

The Creek War was over, and the mighty Creek nation never again posed a threat to the United States. Weatherford became a successful and prosperous plantation owner in Monroe County, Alabama, dying in 1824. His nemesis, Andrew Jackson, went on to become seventh president of the United States and author of the Indian Removal Act of 1830, which eventually forced not only the Creeks but Jackson's Cherokee allies as well to surrender all of their eastern lands and resettle west of the Mississippi River.

THE BATTLE OF NEW ORLEANS

Louisiana, 1815

Whenever the War of 1812 is discussed, the clash that usually comes to the forefront of conversation is the Battle of New Orleans. The conflict occurred on January 8, 1815—ironically, two weeks after representatives of the United States and Great Britain signed the peace treaty ending the war. However, neither opposing commander, General Andrew Jackson nor British General Sir Edward Pakenham, was aware of the fact.

America's second conflict with Great Britain had officially begun on June 18, 1812, when a reluctant Congress voted seventy-nine to forty-nine in the House of Representatives and nineteen to thirteen in the Senate to declare war. Affairs between the two nations had been deteriorating for several years, precipitated primarily by the British policy of impressment, or seizure, of American sailors on the high seas. At the time, the British navy was experiencing a heavy loss of its own sailors through desertion. In order to reduce its attrition rate, the Royal Navy implemented a policy of searching American vessels on the high seas for its runaway sailors. The U.S. government protested the action, especially since, in many cases, the British not only reclaimed their own subjects, but seized numerous American citizens as well. When a group of young, newly elected congressmen known as the War Hawks—John C. Calhoun of South Carolina, Felix Grundy of Tennessee, and Henry Clay of Kentucky—vocalized their grave concerns over this violation of maritime law, they quickly turned the nation's attention away from the more conservative peace factions and set the stage for the ensuing conflict.

In July, following the declaration of war, General William Hull, the governor of Michigan Territory, invaded Canada. Fearing that his communications with Detroit would be cut by the British, he quickly retreated across the border after learning that Fort Michilimackinac had surrendered peaceably. On August 16, Detroit surrendered to British troops, and Michigan and the upper Mississippi River valley fell temporarily under British control.

During the course of the conflict, considerable action took place around the Great Lakes and along the eastern seaboard. Finally, on August 25, 1813, the British invaded Washington and burned both the Capitol and the President's House. Eighteen days later, redcoats attacked Baltimore, but the success of Fort McHenry in protecting the city doomed the attempt to failure.

The city of New Orleans was the prize in the South. British military planners determined that it was absolutely necessary to capture the port at the mouth of the Mississippi River so they could exercise complete control over the stream, thereby restricting use of the river or the port facilities at New Orleans to inland American farmers who had no other outlet for their products.

At New Orleans, during a two-week period in late 1814 and early 1815, besieged Americans, under the command of Andrew Jackson, confronted a superior British army led by Sir Edward Pakenham. Jackson deployed his army of Tennesseans, Kentuckians, pirates, blacks, Indians, and Creoles along the dried-up Rodriguez Canal. Heavy British artillery fire failed to dislodge them, so Pakenham ordered his 5,400 veteran soldiers of the Crown to attack Jackson's defenses head-on. The British troops became easy targets for the rag-tag American army, and the Battle of New Orleans was won in thirty minutes. More than two thousand British soldiers were killed during the brief encounter, while Jackson lost only thirteen troops.

The two commanders at New Orleans were as different as daylight and dark. Jackson, a product of the wild frontier, had just recently distinguished himself by overcoming the Creek Indians in Alabama. He had moved to Nashville in the late 1780s and, after filling several public offices, the forty-seven-year-old veteran was now a major-general in the U.S. Army.

Pakenham, on the other hand, had been brought up in a well-to-do family and had been trained in the classic European school of warfare. He was rudely awakened by the unorthodox methods of fighting displayed by Jackson's Tennesseans and other troops. Organized, well-disciplined, "follow-the-leader" soldiers had no place in the swamps of Louisiana, a point well taken by Pakenham as he observed hundreds of his red-coated troops fall to the ground in heaps before the blistering fire of the Americans. A few minutes into the fight, Pakenham himself was killed. Years later, Jackson recalled the event and related the circumstances of his adversary's death:

> *I heard a single rifle shot from a group of country carts*
> *we had been using, and a moment thereafter I saw*
> *Pakenham reel and pitch out of his saddle. . . . I did*
> *not know where General Pakenham was lying or I*
> *should have sent to him, or gone to him in person, to*

offer any service in my power to render. I was told he
lived two hours after he was hit.

The affair at New Orleans catapulted Andrew Jackson into the public limelight. Theodore Roosevelt, in his maritime study, *Naval War of 1812*, wrote:

> *The American soldiers deserve great credit for doing so*
> *well; but greater credit still belongs to Andrew Jackson,*
> *who, with his cool hand, stands out in history as the*
> *ablest general the United States produced from the out-*
> *break of the Revolution down to the beginning of the*
> *Great Rebellion.*

The War of 1812 lasted thirty months. Despite the large loss of life and property on both sides, the conflict accomplished little, and when it was finally over, the strained relationship between the two combatants was no different than what it was before.

DENMARK VESEY'S SLAVE REVOLT

South Carolina, 1822

In the July 3, 1822, issue of the *Charleston* [South Carolina] *Courier*— just above a listing of the Charleston Bible Society's officers for the year 1822–23—appeared the following:

> *Execution.—DENMARK VESEY, (a free black man)*
> *ROLLA, BATTEAU, NED, PETER, and JESSE*
> *(slaves) convicted of an attempt to raise an insurrection*
> *in this State, were executed, pursuant to sentence, yes-*
> *terday morning, between the hours of 6 and 8 o'clock.*

Although Charleston's city fathers had attempted to keep the execution, and particularly the burial site, of Vesey and his associates a secret, contemporary accounts indicated that very large numbers of both white and black citizens of Charleston were on hand to observe the entire proceedings.

Just who was Denmark Vesey, and why was it so important for city officials to clandestinely execute and bury him, preferably without the knowledge of the citizenry of Charleston? Although today very few Americans, including Southerners, have ever heard of the man, according to his biographer, David Robertson, he organized the most elaborate and well-planned slave insurrection in the history of the United States. Had it succeeded, it also would have been the most violent. Nine years before Nat Turner's slave revolt in Virginia's Tidewater district, and thirty-seven years before John Brown's raid at Harpers Ferry, Vesey planned to seize the U.S. arsenal and ships at harbor in Charleston, then the fifth-largest city in the nation. In preparation for this attack, he recruited as many as nine thousand slaves to his cause.

Perhaps to understand who Vesey *was not* is the best way to define who he was. First, he was not a young buck in his twenties or thirties who went around Charleston spewing hatred toward white citizens, but rather around fifty-five years old when he was arrested for fomenting the revolt. He was not a slave, but a freedman, meaning that he had purchased his freedom from his master (in his case twenty-two years earlier, with funds won on a raffle ticket). He was not a vagrant who lived in a shantytown, but rather an accomplished carpenter whose services were constantly sought by the white elite of Charleston and who lived in the same neighborhood as the city's mayor and South Carolina's governor. Finally, he was not ignorant and, although the nature of his early schooling is not known, he spoke and wrote fluently in English and French, in addition to speaking Spanish, Creole, and several other languages.

Denmark Vesey had formerly been a slave of Bermuda-born Captain Joseph Vesey, a slave trader who moved to Charleston around 1783, bringing the sixteen-year-old Denmark, then named Telemaque, with him. When the captain purchased the youngster two years earlier, he favored the boy and soon became quite partial to him. However, Vesey eventually sold Telemaque to a plantation owner in present-day Haiti, who, upon Captain Vesey's later return to the island, declared that the boy suffered from epilepsy and would not work in the cane fields. Vesey returned the purchase price, bestowed the name "Denmark Vesey" upon the slave, and assigned him the duties of being his assistant.

In 1815 an African Methodist Episcopal (AME) church was organized in Charleston in protest against white congregations that, according to the blacks of the city, had unfairly treated them. Local AME membership quickly grew to nearly 4,500 members, both slaves and freemen. Denmark Vesey, now nearly fifty years old, had originally attended the socially prominent Second Presbyterian church, but soon joined the AME church and became a class leader in Bible instruction. He became increasingly intrigued by the primitive African influences taught in the church, and sometime during this period, around late 1817 or early 1818, he developed the genesis of a massive slave revolt that would free his people once and for all. According to an acquaintance, Denmark "tried to prove from it [the Bible] that slavery and bondage is against the Bible." Vesey often referred to Moses and his emancipation from Egypt of the chosen people. He suggested that slavery in Charleston might someday be remedied as described in Joshua 6:21, "And they utterly destroyed all that were in the city, both man and woman, both young and old."

For the next five years, Vesey became more and more convinced that a slave rebellion among Charleston's black population was not only doable, but would be successful if it could be kept a secret from the white community until the day came to strike. He recruited heavily from not only the AME congregation, but also the farmworkers laboring on rural plantations in the region. With the smoothness and glib of a modern-day TV preacher, he convinced his anxious listeners that, when the revolt finally got under way, it would receive support from outside the United States, namely Haiti—or, if they preferred, they could escape to either Haiti or Africa, where they could live out their lives in freedom.

By May 1822 all appeared ready for the revolt to occur. Vesey chose a date, July 14, for his followers to loot, pillage, and kill throughout Charleston. But then on May 25 occurred an incident, seemingly innocent at first, that threw the future of the revolt into extreme jeopardy. A house slave named Prioleau, who belonged to an influential white family of the same name, was stopped on the street by a black man he had never seen before and asked if he was aware of "something serious that was about to take place." When Prioleau replied in the negative, the stranger declared, "Why, we are determined to shake off our bondage, and for this purpose we stand on a firm foundation," adding that if the slave would join him, he would "show you the man, who has the list of names, who will take yours down." Prioleau, terrified by what he had just heard, reported the incident to his master, but not until five days later.

The black man who had attempted to recruit Prioleau on the street was identified as William Paul. He was arrested and was soon coerced into telling authorities everything they wanted to know about the upcoming revolt. He gave up the names of many of Vesey's top lieutenants, but not that of Vesey himself. By June 12, however, city and jail officials, after interviewing other blacks in town and convinced that Paul's story was just a yarn, dismissed it.

The recent action disturbed Vesey, and he decided to advance the date of the rebellion before the white community and authorities discovered the plot. The new time for the uprising would be midnight on June 16. But on June 14 the proposed revolt's secrecy was finally breached for good when another slave reported to his master that he, too, had been propositioned to join the uprising. Telling his owner that "a public disturbance was contemplated by the blacks and that not a moment should be lost in informing the constituted authorities," the frightened slave continued, "The succeeding Sunday, the 16th, at twelve o'clock at night, was the period fixed for the rising."

When the governor and mayor were advised of this latest development, they called out four hundred state militia, many of them mounted and all heavily armed, and ordered them to patrol the city's streets. Within hours, rumors of the slave revolt spread throughout Charleston and the surrounding countryside, and whites everywhere were on their guard. On June 15, when Vesey observed unusually busy military activity on the streets, he contemplated delaying the uprising. Later in the day, his mind was made up for him when he sent a messenger to the outlying plantations with instructions to rally the slaves there into rebellion, but the man returned and advised Vesey that he had never been able to break through the cordon of guards around the city. As midnight Saturday, June 15, slipped into Sunday, June 16, dead calm hovered over the city.

When dawn cracked on June 16, city officials began rounding up suspects. Although, even at this late date, Vesey's name had still not surfaced, by the following weekend the freedman was very much a suspect and he was arrested and taken to jail. His interrogators were shocked and later declared that he had "enjoyed so much the confidence of the whites, that when he was accused, the charge was . . . discredited . . . and not until the proof of his guilt had become too strong to be doubted" would anyone believe that he was involved.

The trial of Vesey and several of the rebellion's ringleaders was begun immediately, and on June 27 they listened as the judge pronounced them guilty and sentenced them to death, their punishment to occur on July 2. Vesey went to the gallows with no comments, no apologies, no confession of wrongdoing, and no cry for clemency. In his ruling the judge had succinctly summarized the entire failed slave revolt, masterminded by this well-respected member of Charleston black society, when he wrote that Vesey had "artfully" employed

> *every principle which could operate upon the mind*
> *of man. . . . Religion, hope, fear, and deception were*
> *resorted to as the occasion required. All were told, and*
> *many believed, that God approved of their designs;*
> *those whose fears would have restrained them, were*
> *forced to yield by threats of death; those whom pru-*
> *dence and foresight induced them to pause, were*
> *cheered with the assurance that assistance from Santo*
> *Domingo and Africa were at hand.*

FRANCES WRIGHT'S DREAM

Tennessee, 1826

The early 1800s found many utopian colonies operating across the United States. An early one was Robert Owens's New Harmony experiment, founded in 1825 in the farmlands of extreme Southwestern Indiana. A lesser-known community was Nashoba, organized just a few miles from Memphis, Tennessee, and the banks of the Mississippi River.

Nashoba's founding genius was a British woman named Frances (Fanny) Wright. Born in 1795 in Dundee, Scotland, Fanny was orphaned at a young age and raised by English relatives. Well-educated for a female of the period, Wright soon fell under the influence of French materialism philosophies, and during her early twenties she became an outspoken disciple of utopianism, women's rights, free love, and other radical—for the times, at least—movements.

When Fanny was twenty-three years old, she and her sister, Camilla, traveled to the United States. What the two self-declared reformers found in the towns and countryside of rural America was

a ready-made platform for their philosophies and beliefs. Fanny
unsuccessfully tried her hand at writing and producing a play in
New York City in 1819, the plot of which gravitated around Swiss
independence. Two years later she published a popular book titled
Views of Society and Manners in America, a study that captured the
attention of European radical reformers, including the French hero
of the American Revolution, the Marquis de Lafayette.

Lafayette's influence on the Wright sisters led them to for-
mulate and launch a new enterprise in the United States. During
her earlier American travels, Fanny had never toured the South,
primarily because of her abhorrence of slavery. Now she decided
that she would visit the region and become a spokeswoman for
abolition, and establish a colony for freed slaves as well. Edd Winfield Parks, a prominent Tennessee historian and biographer, best
described the project's mission when he wrote in 1932 that Fanny's
proposed utopia was to

> *educate and . . . emancipate the slaves. But the work*
> *must be done gradually. Her . . . colony would be based*
> *on a system of cooperative labor, the slaves bought in*
> *whole families. Within five years, she figured, the labor*
> *of the slaves would pay for their original cost, including*
> *six per cent interest on the capital, and for their keep.*
> *In this period the older slaves could be taught a trade,*
> *taught at least to read, to figure, and to write: the chil-*
> *dren could be given a complete rudimentary education.*
> *Absolute and immediate abolition might be productive*
> *of great evil: this gradual emancipation, with careful*
> *teaching . . . would benefit not only the slaves, but the*

white people. White immigrants would take the place
of the negroes, who might be colonized in Haiti, Texas,
or California, where they could work out a civiliza-
tion of their own. Apparently it never occurred to Miss
Wright that within a few years Texas and California
would be integral parts of the United States, vital fac-
tors in the menacing issue of slavery.

In September 1825, with grandiose ideas in her mind and
$17,000 in her pocketbook, Fanny Wright arrived in Nashville to
meet with General Andrew Jackson, who was, at the time, active
in land speculation in the far western part of Tennessee. Jackson—
along with his onetime law partner, John Overton, and General
James Winchester—had founded Memphis in Shelby County on
the banks of the Mississippi River only six years earlier. Now "Old
Hickory" was anxious to dispose of as much Shelby County land as
he could. He directed Fanny to his friends William Lawrence and
William A. Davis, from whom the colonizer purchased three hundred acres of marshy woodland along the Wolf River. According to
historian Parks, Wright christened her new home "Nashoba, the old
Chickasaw name for wolf."

Within six months of the land purchase, the Nashoba colony
started off with a bang. Two large log houses were built: Fanny,
Camilla, and the sisters' white followers occupied one, while the
several slaves they had bought in Nashville set up housekeeping in
the other. During the next year, more land was acquired and cleared,
several other cabins were built, and Fanny came down with a severe
case of malaria. In an attempt to recuperate as rapidly as possible,
she was forced to move north to the cooler climate of New Albany,
Indiana. In her absence, Nashoba fell on hard times.

Sister Camilla, who had taken over the job of teaching both young and old slaves, found her subjects difficult to deal with. Little work was done by anybody, and the project just rocked along, making little progress for the next several months. One year after its founding, a disappointed visitor described Nashoba's surroundings as "second-rate land, and scarcely a hundred acres of it cleared: three or four squared log houses, and a few cabins for the slaves, the only buildings; slaves released from the fear of the lash, working indolently."

Fanny recuperated and returned to Europe, hoping to drum up support and additional dollars for her noble Tennessee experiment. In her absence the direction of the operations took a different turn, leaving the poor, uneducated slaves the real victims of the misdirected project. The original bylaws of Nashoba stipulated that before a slave could be emancipated, the fruits of his labor must pay the organization a total of $6,000 plus his living expenses. Now, to make matters worse, severe restrictions were placed upon those in bondage, making many wonder whether slavery itself was not a better fate. Two of the rules were particularly offensive to the slaves. One dictated that they "not be allowed to receive money, clothing, food, or indeed anything whatever from any person resident at, or visiting this place," while another one demanded that the slaves "not be permitted to eat elsewhere than at the public meals."

Fanny revisited Nashoba in 1828, full of fresh vigor and new expectations for her slave colony. But gradually the malarial climate, the lack of money, and a decided cooling of the fervor originally demonstrated by the Wright sisters closed the doors on the gone-astray utopian colony. Fanny spent a final season in Tennessee, freed all the remaining slaves, and moved to New Harmony, Indiana. In her memoirs, published in 1844, she admitted failure, and that "for the first time she bowed her head in humility before the omnipotence of collective humanity."

Fanny lived for another twenty-two years after her failure at Nashoba. During that period she traveled the American lecture tour, wrote widely on her radical philosophies, married, gave birth to a daughter, and separated from her husband. She lived in retirement in Cincinnati, Ohio, until her death in 1852. Perhaps the *American Cyclopedia of Biography* best described this courageous, if not somewhat misguided, woman when its biographer wrote, "She was benevolent, unselfish, eccentric, and fearless."

ANDREW JACKSON'S
BRUSH WITH DEATH

District of Columbia, 1835

The weather in Washington, D.C., was cold and blustery when President Andrew Jackson stepped from his carriage at the east entrance of the U.S. Capitol. It was January 30, 1835, and the soon-to-be-sixty-eight-year-old president was on his way to a funeral. Accompanied by Missouri Senator Thomas Hart Benton, Secretary of the Navy Mahlon Dickerson, and Secretary of the Treasury Levi Woodbury, Jackson quickly made his way up the stairs and entered the Capitol Rotunda, glad to be out of the fierce wind. His small entourage then made its way down the marbled hallway to the chamber of the House of Representatives, wherein the body of U.S. Congressman Warren R. Davis of South Carolina lay in state.

After viewing Davis's remains and paying his respects to the family, President Jackson and his party returned to the Rotunda and prepared to leave the Capitol for the short trip up Pennsylvania Avenue to the White House. As Jackson, Dickerson, and Woodbury exited the building, a man jumped out of the crowd, pointed a pistol at the president's heart, and pulled the trigger. The weapon was supplied with a percussion lock, and when the hammer fell on the cap, the cap itself exploded but the powder charge failed. The frantic, would-be assassin shoved a second pistol toward Jackson, but miraculously that one failed to fire as well.

Upon hearing the explosion of the two caps, President Jackson took the offensive and, in an instant, the tall, unscathed Tennessean—ailing, but still feisty, and with his walking cane raised above his head—lunged toward the shooter, ready to extract vengeance. Meanwhile, Secretary Woodbury struck a blow at the attacker, while a nearby navy lieutenant knocked him to the floor. Bystanders captured and held the man until law enforcement officers arrived and arrested him.

An inquiry into the incident was immediately launched. The marshal of the District of Columbia questioned whether the suspect might suffer from mental illness, and he assigned two highly respected physicians to carefully examine the man. Their two-hour-long investigation revealed that the shooter was an unemployed house painter by the name of Richard Lawrence. He refused to give his age, but was determined to be "young." Actually, he was probably around thirty-five years old at the time. He did admit that he was originally from England and that he had migrated to the United States as a child. He had been out of work for some time, a fact that had caused him "much pecuniary embarrassment."

During the course of his erratic ramblings, Lawrence told his questioners that "his family had been wrongfully deprived of the crown of England." He also admitted that the idea of killing the president had haunted him for some time. He had even visited the White House the previous week and had a brief audience with Jackson. At the time, he had demanded that the president issue him a bank draft so that he could return to England and reclaim his inheritance.

Jackson spurned the idea, intimating that he was much too busy to discuss such matters.

During Lawrence's questioning, it was clear that he was quite disconcerted that his pair of pistols had misfired. He told authorities that he often shot both weapons and that they had never before malfunctioned. He had loaded them with fresh powder several days earlier, but had rammed the balls home with a pencil instead of a ramrod. When the two pistols were later recharged and tested by interrogators, both of them fired readily, driving their projectiles through a one-inch-thick plank at thirty feet.

When questioned why he wanted to kill the president, Lawrence went into a lengthy, disjointed diatribe about his personal woes, his extended period of unemployment, how it was Jackson's fault that he had lost his job to begin with, and his contention that Jackson was "a tyrant." Continuing, Lawrence believed "the President to be the source of all his difficulties," and he admitted that "he was still fixed in his purpose to kill him, and if his successor pursued the same course, to put him out of the way also."

He went to the Capitol that day, Lawrence told his interrogators, because he knew that President Jackson was going to pay his respects to the deceased congressman from South Carolina. He admitted to being in the Rotunda when Jackson's party first arrived, but that he refrained from shooting then because he did not want to disrupt the funeral proceedings. During the entire incident, he only became apprehensive when the second pistol misfired and he saw Jackson rushing him with his cane, which he feared contained a sword.

Members of the physicians' panel found that Lawrence was mentally impaired and that he was at peace with himself for his heinous actions. In fact, he anticipated no punishment for his deed. Adding his authority to the physicians' opinion that the painter was insane, President Jackson's friend and protégé Thomas Hart Benton later wrote, "It is clearly to be seen from this medical examination of the man, that this attempted assassination of the President, was one of those cases of which history presents many instances—a diseased mind acted upon by a general outcry against a public man."

The following March, Lawrence's case was heard before the Circuit Court of the District of Columbia, where even the prosecutor, Francis Scott Key, composer of the national anthem, agreed to an acquittal. The painter was declared incompetent and sentenced to spend the rest of his life in a mental institution. When the Government Hospital for the Insane opened in Washington, D.C., in 1855, he was transferred to that facility, where he died on June 13, 1861.

FIGHTING THE SEMINOLES

Florida, 1835–42

The Seminole Indians of Florida were and are a consortium of several indigenous tribes who banded together, probably in the late 1700s. Their population increased greatly at the end of the Creek War of 1813–14, when thousands of refugee Creek Indians from neighboring Alabama and Georgia fled to the more remote regions of Florida. From time to time, runaway slaves contributed their blood to the extent that the tribe eventually became a mixture of Muskogean, non-Muskogean, and black peoples.

On May 28, 1830, President Andrew Jackson signed the Removal Act, calling for the expulsion to the West of all Indian tribes living east of the Mississippi River. The edict, of course, included the Florida tribes. Two years later James Gadsden, on orders from Secretary of War Lewis Cass, met with a group of friendly Seminoles at Payne's Landing, located between Lakes Orange and George in north-central Florida. There, in exchange for less than $20,000 in cash and trade goods, the tribesmen signed a treaty whereby they relinquished a huge tract of Florida territory to the United States government. The cession, added to the Seminoles' earlier transfer of land to the government at Moultrie Creek in September 1823, resulted in the entire present-day state of Florida falling under the domain of the United States.

Many Seminoles, however, were unhappy about the treaty signing at Payne's Landing. They said that the papers were signed by tribal members who had no authority to give away the land and, consequently, little was achieved toward moving the natives to the West. During the next three years, government agents met several times with various tribal leaders, attempting to get consensus on the Payne's Landing agreement and to begin the relocation process. During the spring of 1835, at one of the sessions held by Indian agent Wiley Thompson, a young Indian jumped forward and plunged his knife into the treaty papers lying on the negotiating table. He was Osceola, not yet a chief but an outspoken Creek who adamantly refused to sanction the removal of his adopted tribe. Standing defiantly before his white adversaries, he declared:

> *My brothers! The white man says I shall go and he will send people to make me go; but I have a rifle, and I have some powder and some lead. I say, we must not leave our homes and lands. If any of our people want to go west we won't let them; and I tell them they are our enemies, and we will treat them so, for the great spirit will protect us.*

Agent Thompson signaled for soldiers to arrest the angry Osceola and place him in custody. The following day, the Indian sent a message to Thompson that he would sign the treaty after all, but as soon as his pen was put to paper, he bolted into the nearby wilderness, determined to carry his battle on.

Within weeks of Osceola's escape, violence commenced on the Florida frontier. White villages were raided by hostile Seminoles, while friendly Indians pleaded with the federal government for protection from their warlike kinsmen. By the end of December 1835, Osceola had capitalized on an opportunity to ambush and kill the hated Agent Thompson, while another band of Seminoles annihilated one hundred American soldiers, under the command of Major Francis Dade, in the interior. On the last day of the year, Osceola himself led a strong contingent of warriors against a large force consisting of five hundred Florida militiamen and three hundred regular army troops near the Withlacoochee River. In the carnage, sixty-three soldiers were either killed or wounded, as the victorious Seminoles faded into the dense forests.

For the next seven years the war dragged on, touching the lives of all Floridians—Indian, white, and black. It affected towns and villages from the Atlantic Ocean to the Gulf Coast and from the Everglades to the Georgia border. Distressed East Floridians—either dismissing the wrongs that had been committed against the Seminoles by the United States government or, at least, preferring to forget about them—begged an inept Congress for assistance, writing:

> *Suddenly, when prosperity and success were crowning their [the American settlers'] labors, and the country was at last rising superior to the difficulties and accidents which had for years embarrassed its advancement, they find themselves surrounded by a savage foe, bearing the firebrand and tomahawk through the land with unrestrained fury, and the country enveloped in the horrors of a warfare at which the imagination of civilized man revolts, and humanity sickens. They have been forced*

almost universally to abandon their habitations and
their property to the licentious rage of the enemy, and flee
with their families to places of temporary security.

In many respects the protracted war was a preview of events that would plague the American army in Vietnam 125 years later. Ghost fighters appearing out of the subtropical forests and swamps would strike an army command, wrack their destruction, then disappear into the shadows. The Seminoles, like the Viet Cong, were masters of guerilla warfare, and the carnage heaped upon the American army and the citizens of Florida proved it. One young soldier fighting in Florida wrote:

For nearly two hundred miles, we passed through an
unknown region, cutting through dense hummocks,
passing innumerable cypress-swamps and pine barrens
. . . and, for the last three days, wading . . . up to our
necks in water. Our privations have not been less than
our fatigue, the men being almost naked, and one third
of them destitute of shoes.

In addition to trying the patience of the foot soldier, the war proved to be embarrassing to the War Department, despite the fact that the names of the commanders and senior field officers assigned at one time or another to the Florida campaign read like a Who's Who of American military history: Edmund Pendleton Gaines, Duncan Clinch, Winfield Scott, Thomas S. Jesup, Zachary Taylor, William Selby Harney, Alexander Macomb, Walker K. Armistead, and William J. Worth.

The military commanders were befuddled: How was the army ever going to defeat this hit-and-run enemy? Stooping to treachery was one option, and that is exactly what General Jesup did in October 1837, when he invited Osceola, under a flag of truce, to parley. When the Creek warrior arrived at the American camp, he was arrested and sent to Fort Marion at Saint Augustine, where he died the following January.

In time—more in spite of than because of the American army's actions—the Florida War ended, but the conflict had cost the U.S. government $20 million and deployed 30,000 soldiers, with 1,500 of them killed in action and many hundreds more either wounded or stricken by disease. Most of the Seminoles were deported to present-day Oklahoma, thus fulfilling Andrew Jackson's pledge to send all of the eastern tribes West, but a few fled into the remote wilderness of the Everglades, where their descendants still reside.

The horrible war of 1835–42 is sometimes called the Second Seminole War. Actually, there was one war with the Seminoles prior to the second and one afterwards. The First Seminole War was conducted during 1816–18, with General Andrew Jackson the primary player. Its main outcome was Spain's relinquishment of the remainder of its American possessions lying east of the Mississippi River, thus putting Florida into the American fold.

In 1856, when several American oystermen were killed by Seminoles in the Florida Keys, the Third Seminole War began. By this time Florida had been admitted to the Union, and the army quickly deployed soldiers to quash the uprising. William Selby Harney, veteran of the Second Seminole War, was dispatched to the scene, and after nearly two years, he succeeded in overpowering the few-hundred-member Seminole resistance. As historian George Rollie Adams wrote in his comprehensive biography of Harney, "The Third Seminole War represented one last major demonstration of the federal government's inhumane Indian removal policy and highlighted once again the army's difficulties in dealing with native warriors' unconventional fighting methods."

JOHN THOMPSON'S
HORRIFIC ORDEAL

Florida, 1836

John Thompson was a pretty lonely fellow as, night after night, month after month, he manned the lighthouse perched upon Key Biscayne, a tiny island just off the coast of present-day Miami, Florida. The lighthouse had been built ten years earlier and stood sixty-five feet above the ground. Its five-feet-thick brick walls at ground level tapered to two feet at the top and provided the strength required for the building's extreme weight. Crowning the tower was a large lantern, fed by oil, which created the beacon that could be seen by errant seamen for miles. Situated around the base of the lighthouse were a dwelling that Thompson occupied, a separate kitchen, and several outbuildings.

Except for the old black man who helped Thompson with his tiresome vigil, residents in the area were few and far between and seldom were seen. Of course, a war had been going on for months with neighboring Seminole Indians, which explained why most folks exercised caution when it came to not getting caught out in the swampy wilderness that covered extreme southern Florida.

July 23, 1836, dawned clear, hot, and humid for Thompson, and the day gave every indication that it would hold no more excitement than days gone by. It is doubtful that the light keeper had received news yet that during the previous March, way out in Texas, a small contingent of Americans had been annihilated by the Mexican army. However, he no doubt would have been aware that on December 31 of the previous year, the Seminole chief Osceola and a group of his followers, nursing a hatred for all Americans, had engaged an army of eight hundred regular army troops and militiamen on the Withlacoochee River, some two hundred miles to the northwest.

The day had indeed been uneventful until around 4:00 p.m., when Thompson—walking between the kitchen and the dwelling and making silent plans for the evening's work in the tiny enclosure at the top of the lighthouse—was confronted by a sizable party of Seminole tribesmen. Frightened, he made a run for the lighthouse, calling for his black companion all the time. Several Seminoles fired, their balls slashing through the white man's loose-fitting clothing and a few lodging in the door to the lighthouse.

Fortunately, both Thompson and his friend made it safely inside the lighthouse, when the Indians started beating at the door. Thompson stationed his companion downstairs while he climbed to the second floor, armed with three muskets loaded with ball and buckshot, where he "discharged my muskets in succession among them, which put them in some confusion." The Indians were persistent and unyielding, however, and according to the lighthouse keeper:

> *For the second time, they began their horrid yells, and*
> *in a minute no sash or glass was left at the window,*
> *for they vented their rage at that spot. I fired at them*
> *from some of the other windows and from the top of*

the lighthouse; in fact, I fired whenever I could get an
Indian for a mark. I kept them from the lighthouse
until dark.

As pitch blackness loomed over the island, the Seminoles continued their unrelenting attack, eventually setting fire to the inside of the lighthouse, including Thompson's makeshift bedroom where he rested during the long nights of vigil. Stray musket and rifle balls penetrated the metal tanks that held the 225 gallons of oil that fed the lantern. The flames spread quickly, fed by the oil and the resin-rich yellow pine flooring that lined the lighthouse.

Thompson then took drastic action. He and his friend retreated to the very top of the tower with a keg of powder and one musket. Then, he cut down the stairs that had carried the two men to the top, effectively isolating them in the lantern room with no means of escape. As the flames eventually made their way to the top of the tower and into the lantern room, the victims tried crouching on the outside platform that surrounded the top of the tower. "My clothes were on fire," Thompson declared, "but to move from the place where I was would be instant death from their rifles."

The lighthouse keeper then hurled the keg of powder directly into the flames, the explosion shaking the entire building from top to bottom. The old black man shouted that he was wounded, then died. Thompson's only avenue of escape now was to jump off the top of the tower and take a chance on surviving the sixty-five-foot fall, although he was already wounded six times. As he pondered his predicament, he was mysteriously persuaded to not jump after all, but instead went back inside the burning building and crouched down to await his fate.

As the conflagration began to die down, the Indians, believing that Thompson was dead, ransacked the dwelling house, the kitchen, and what was left of the lighthouse. When morning came, Thompson watched from his perch high above the beach as forty or fifty Seminoles loaded up his boat with the spoils of victory and departed the premises, some aboard the skiff and some on foot. Poor Thompson knew that he was in a real predicament, writing later:

> *I was now almost as bad off as before—a burning fever on me, my feet shot to pieces, no clothes to cover me, nothing to eat or drink, a hot sun overhead, a dead man by my side, no friend near or any to expect, and placed between seventy and eighty feet from the earth, and no chance of getting down. My situation was truly horrible.*

At around noon the same day, Thompson thought he saw a boat on the horizon and signaled it. A few minutes later, he watched as his skiff and two other boats pulled up to the landing. The entourage turned out to be members of the United States Navy, who had recovered the skiff after the Indians had stripped it of everything of value. The men had heard the explosion of the previous day and had made their way to the lighthouse to check on any survivors. Unable to reach Thompson, still positioned high in the tower, the men promised to return the following day.

When they arrived the next morning, several attempts were made to get a rope up to Thompson, and success finally was realized when a length of twine tied to a ramrod was fired from a musket and landed near the stranded lighthouse keeper. The rescuers then sent up a pulley, which Thompson made fast to a piece of ironwork in the tower. The twine was replaced by a two-inch rope run through the pulley, whereby two sailors hoisted themselves up the wall of the tower and assisted the severely wounded man to earth.

After administering all the first aid they could, the sailors carried Thompson to Charleston, South Carolina, for further treatment and recuperation. There he wrote a letter to the editor of the *Charleston Courier,* wherein he gave a short, but complete, narrative of his harrowing experiences. In the letter he thanked one and all who had cared for him and assured them that, although he was "a cripple, I can eat my allowance and walk about without the use of a cane."

Despite the continued hostile Seminole activity in the area, John Thompson's lighthouse was eventually rebuilt at the same location, and its bright beam was redirected toward the Atlantic Ocean for the first time in 1846. The installation was decommissioned in 1878.

THE TRAIL OF TEARS

Georgia, 1838

Winfield Scott carefully lowered his lumbering six-foot, three-inch frame into a rickety camp chair inside his makeshift tent located amid the lush, green mountains of North Georgia. Scott, a major-general and second-highest-ranking officer in the United States Army, did not look forward to his most recent orders. He had only recently returned from a long campaign against the Seminole Indians deep in the sweltering swamps of Florida, and prior to that had been passed over for promotion to commanding general of the entire army. Now, on the eve of yet another controversial assignment, it seemed to the fifty-one-year-old warrior that he always ended up with the most undesirable and unwanted duty.

It was spring 1838, and General Scott had only recently been ordered to Cherokee country to forcibly remove that advanced and totally assimilated tribe to lands beyond the Mississippi River. For eight years now—ever since President Andrew Jackson signed the Indian Removal Act—federal authorities had attempted to expel the fifteen thousand members of the proud Cherokee nation from their traditional lands in Georgia, Tennessee, and North Carolina. Soon after the passage of the Removal Act, the tribe's chief, John Ross, had avoided the inevitable by taking the U.S. government to task. When the Cherokees' case was favorably ruled on by the U.S. Supreme Court in 1831, President Jackson's response had been, "John Marshall [the court's chief justice] has made his decision. Now let him enforce it."

To complicate matters, Major John Ridge, who aspired to become chief of the Cherokee nation, had signed a treaty in 1835 at New Echota that relinquished to the government all remaining Cherokee lands east of the Mississippi River. Questions were immediately raised as to the treaty's legality since only a small segment of the Cherokee leadership had approved it. Nevertheless, federal officials pointed to the controversial document as their authority to demand the Cherokees' expulsion.

Now, time had nearly run out for John Ross and his stalwart followers, who had no desire to relocate beyond the Mississippi River. General Scott and seven thousand U.S. troops had only recently arrived in Cherokee country to see that the government's will was done. Stockades had been built to house the Cherokees after they were forced to leave their homes and farmsteads, and supplies—one pound of flour and a half pound of bacon daily for each "prisoner"— had been gathered to distribute among the disheartened Indians.

Scott carefully pulled a letter from a packet of documents, mindfully unfolded it, and once again read his controversial orders:

> *From recent intelligence received from the Govern-*
> *ment agents among the Cherokees, it is apprehended*
> *that the mass of the nation, under some delusion, does*
> *not intend to remove to the country provided for them*

under the stipulations of the treaty. . . . You will,
therefore, repair, without unnecessary delay, to Athens,
in Tennessee, or to any other point in your opinion
most convenient for making your arrangements. Orders
have been given for the 4th regiment of artillery, the
4th regiment of infantry, and six companies of the 2d
dragoons, now in Florida, to repair, as early as practi-
cable, to the Cherokee country. . . . You are authorized
to call on the Governors of the States of Tennessee,
North Carolina, Georgia, and Alabama, for such mili-
tia and volunteer force, not exceeding 4,000, in addi-
tion to the regular forces, as you may deem necessary.

Scott closed his eyes, thought for a moment, then reached across his field desk and plucked the feathered quill pen from its inkwell. Smoothing a long piece of yellowed paper on the rough surface of the desk, the troubled general began to write:

Cherokees! The President of the United States has sent
me with a powerful army, to cause you, in obedience to
the treaty of 1835, to join that part of your people who
are already established in prosperity on the other side of
the Mississippi. Unhappily, the two years which were
allowed for the purpose, you have suffered to pass away
without following, and without making any prepara-
tion to follow; and now, or by the time that this solemn
address shall reach your distant settlements, the emigra-
tion must be commenced in haste, but I hope without

disorder. I have no power, by granting a farther delay,
to correct the error that you have committed. The
full moon of May is already on the wane; and before
another shall have passed away, every Cherokee man,
woman, and child, in those States, must be in motion
to join their brethren in the far West.

For the next several weeks, Scott oversaw the collection of thousands of Cherokees and their forced confinement in the log stockades that had been built to receive them. He admonished his troops to treat the natives with "every possible kindness," warning them that "simple indiscretions, acts of harshness, and cruelty . . . may lead . . . to delays, to impatience, and exasperation, and in the end, to a general war and carnage." The general suggested that "by early and persevering acts of kindness and humanity, it is impossible to doubt that the Indians may soon be induced to confide in the army, and, instead of fleeing to mountains and forest, flock to us for food and clothing."

By summer the long migration of thousands of Cherokees to the land of the setting sun had begun, via two routes. One followed the river system down the Tennessee, Ohio, and Mississippi to the mouth of the Arkansas and up that stream to present-day Oklahoma. In October an overland party, including John Ross himself, started its long journey, trekking through Nashville and across Kentucky and part of Southern Illinois, ferrying over the Mississippi River into Missouri, and then marching to Oklahoma.

About four thousand of the fourteen thousand Indians who traveled the Trail of Tears died en route, including John Ross's wife. Ross himself went on to become a diligent worker for his people in their new homeland, eventually rising to become principal chief of the western branch of the tribe. Major Ridge and his son, John, both parties to the illegal treaty signing at New Echota, were murdered in June 1839 in their new homeland by a group of disgruntled disciples of Ross. Meanwhile, back in Georgia, a few hundred Cherokees escaped the watchful eye of the army and took refuge in the dense forests of the Southern Appalachians, where their descendants still live today.

MEMOIRS OF A NATCHEZ BUSINESSMAN

Mississippi, 1851

Few are the times that researchers have the good fortune to encounter undiscovered narratives about an entire era of American history written by a long-deceased person who experienced the life and times of the period in question. Much rarer is the appearance of a journal whose author was a free black man living in the antebellum South. Such was exactly the case in 1938, however, when Edwin Adams Davis unexpectedly brought to light a treasure trove of previously unknown documents hidden away in a house in downtown Natchez, Mississippi—a house that turned out to be the former home of one William Johnson.

The diary found that long-ago day by Davis was, according to his own words,

> *a significant document in Southern historiography*
> *reveal[ing] important phases of general ante-bellum*
> *Southern life and free Negro-white relations. It also*

pictures the economic and social position of one indi-
vidual, as well as his daily activities, his attitudes
toward the slavery regime, and his thoughts and opin-
ions in local, state, and even national and interna-
tional affairs.

Davis and an associate, William Ransom Hogan, examined and edited the more than two thousand pages of Johnson's handwritten diary for years before they presented it to the public in 1951 as *William Johnson's Natchez: The Ante-Bellum Diary of a Free Negro,* published by Louisiana State University Press. Three years later, *The Barber of Natchez,* a second book about Johnson's interesting life, was released by the two scholars.

At a time when segregation was raging in the South and the momentous U.S. Supreme Court decision in the *Brown v. Board of Education of Topeka* case was still in the future, the publication of books relating to the everyday trials and tribulations of a black man during the years prior to the Civil War was a bit unusual. Feelings among some whites were that the personal lives of black people, be they slave or freed, were at best uninteresting and at worst unimportant to the social fabric of that long-gone era.

Surprisingly, however, despite these attitudes and the fact that Johnson had been dead for a hundred years, he became almost a celebrity among American historians. Manly Wade Wellman, a prolific historical writer of the 1950s, called Johnson the "dark-skinned Pepys," while fellow Southerner Hodding Carter declared that "it is no over-statement to say that this is the most unusual record ever kept in the United States."

Just who was William Johnson, and what drove this onetime slave living in a fine home just one block from the Adams County, Mississippi, courthouse to produce a journal covering sixteen momentous years (1835–51) that witnessed events ranging from the war for Texas independence to the passage of the Fugitive Slave Act and the summons of the Nashville Convention, a proceeding that presaged the Civil War?

He was born, most likely, in Adams County around 1809, the son of a slave woman named Amy and—since he was referred to in court records as "the mulatto boy named William"—a white father. Whether the father was Amy's owner, a white man named William Johnson, is unknown. In any event, Johnson, the slaveholder, freed Amy in 1814, and six years later petitioned the Mississippi General Assembly to free her son, William, as well. William then took his former master's name, and from the date of his freedom onward was known as William Johnson.

Shortly after gaining his freedom, William apprenticed himself to his brother-in-law, James Miller, a free Negro from Philadelphia who soon moved to Natchez, where William quickly established himself as the city's leading barber. When he was nineteen, William moved to Port Gibson, located a few miles north of Natchez on the road to Vicksburg, and opened his own barbershop, which he operated for twenty-two months before returning to Natchez. He was at last an independent businessman, and while at Port Gibson, his earnings from "hair cutting and shaving alone" amounted to $1,094.50.

Arriving back in Natchez, Johnson soon learned that James Miller was about to relocate to New Orleans, and the two men arranged for Johnson to acquire Miller's lease to the barbershop on Main Street and a few adjoining buildings for the sum of $300. Business was good, times were prosperous, and, within three years, Johnson had saved enough money to purchase his shop. Over the next few years, the young barber made improvements to his properties; acquired three slaves; traveled frequently in Mississippi and Louisiana, once journeying to Philadelphia and New York; and participated in several other business endeavors, including the operation of a toy store, a drayage concern, and a real estate rental business. It was during this period of his early entrepreneurship that Johnson started keeping a detailed journal of his business activities, including cash books for income and expenses, records of people he met, and notations about current events.

In 1835 Johnson married Ann Battles, a twenty-year-old freed slave. By then his barbershop was the most patronized in Natchez, and he owned several slaves. His love for the theater and music had become well known throughout the community, and his passion for fine clothes made him a fashion plate among his peers. Things were good for Johnson and his wife, and before his untimely death in 1851, the couple would have ten children together, the last born just one month before Johnson died.

During the 1830s and 1840s, though he maintained his barbershop and opened two others in town, Johnson became interested in farming and land acquisition. In 1845, for a total investment of around $4,000, he purchased three properties totaling 750 acres of fine farm and timber land. To run his agricultural enterprises, he hired white foremen. Although the profits from his farming activities were minimal over the years (he utilized much of the produce from his farms for his own growing family in town), he enjoyed the avocation, combining his love of the rural life with his passion for hunting and fishing.

All through the years, Johnson maintained his propensity for recording in his diary details of life around him. In May 1836 he reported that great news had been received from Texas and that "they [the Texans] had captured St. Anna and killed 500 of his men and had taken abut six hundred of them as prisoners of war." In November 1840 he described a serious fire that broke out in the Natchez-under-the-Hill district and destroyed one of his barbershops, writing,

"Just before Day this morning we were all surprised to hear the alarm of Fire, and I went Down to the Bluff as soon as Possible and there I saw the Last remains of my shop." In March 1843 he detailed a rare snowstorm that struck the city, declaring that "the whole face of the Country was white with Snow and was some 2 or 3 inches deep," adding that Natchez was "perfectly white with Snow and Citizens was throwing Snow balls at Each other in Every direction about the Streets." And he witnessed the visits of many notables of the day, including president-elect Zachary Taylor, former president Andrew Jackson, and the exiled Mexican general, Santa Anna.

On June 16, 1851, William Johnson's life came to an abrupt end. He was riding with one of his sons, along with a slave and a mulatto boy, on the way back to Natchez from his farm when he was ambushed and mortally wounded by three shotgun pellets that pierced his lungs, entered his lower back, and severed his arm. The headline of the newspaper reporting the event proclaimed DREADFUL MURDER IN NATCHEZ and revealed, "On Monday evening last just at dusk, Mr. William Johnson, an esteemed Citizen and long known as the proprietor of the fashionable Barbers' Shop on Main Street, when returning from his Plantation, a few miles from the City, was fired upon and killed from the road side."

Before he died, Johnson revealed the name of his assailant, and within an hour after the ambush a man named Baylor Winn, who owned a neighboring farm, was arrested for the crime. Johnson and Winn had maintained a tenuous friendship over the years, but of late had engaged in heated arguments about their properties' common boundary. Winn was incarcerated for two years and sat through three trials before a jury finally ruled "not guilty," resulting in his release. The primary issue in the trial was that, although a preponderance of testimony revealed that Winn was a freeman with black blood, his lawyers convinced the court that he was actually white with a mixture of Indian blood. Since state law prohibited black people from testifying against whites (and all of the witnesses at the murder scene were black), the jury had no option except to release Winn.

Johnson's widow proudly continued raising her family until she died in 1866, whereupon various children assumed the role of guardian. A grandson, Dr. W. R. Johnston (the family name in the meantime having been changed), was "one of the most highly respected colored citizens of Natchez" when he died in 1938. His widow, Sally, still living in the original Johnson house near the courthouse, was responsible for allowing William Johnson's diary, journal, cash books, receipts, and other personal writings to be made available to the general public.

OPENING SHOTS AT FORT SUMTER

South Carolina, 1861

On December 20, 1860, at a special state convention in Columbia, an ordinance was passed which dissolved the union between South Carolina and the rest of the United States. A few days later the convention requested that the federal government turn over to the state the Charleston Arsenal, along with Forts Moultrie and Sumter and Castle Pinckney. During the last days of December, South Carolina militia occupied Moultrie and Pinckney and seized the arsenal in Charleston.

The month of January 1861 opened and closed with a rapid succession of takeovers by Southern states of federal properties within their boundaries, following the precedent of South Carolina the previous December. The occupation of key U.S. facilities on Southern soil continued until virtually all shore forts and federal arsenals throughout the region were in Southern hands.

The name of Fort Sumter, however—a strong fortress guarding Charleston—was noticeably absent from the list of Southern-occupied installations. Named in honor of Brigadier General Thomas Sumter, the commander of the South Carolina militia during the Revolutionary War, Fort Sumter was begun in 1829. Although built to house 135 heavy-duty cannons, only 60 of the big guns were in place. Hexagonal in shape, the fort—along with its sister structure, neighboring Fort Pulaski at Savannah, Georgia—belonged to a group of fortifications known as the "Third System." Each featured thick walls surrounding a huge interior parade ground, and each wall was not only mounted with long-range firing cannons, but was also internally tiered, with each tier of elevation housing more cannons.

The fort was commanded by Union Major Robert Anderson, a fifty-six-year-old Kentuckian who had graduated from West Point and was a veteran of the Black Hawk, Second Seminole, and Mexican Wars. In November 1860 Anderson was ordered to assume command of Fort Sumter, a task he did not relish since he was married to a Georgian and was not unsympathetic to the institution of slavery. However, his sense of duty to the United States government overrode his other feelings, and he set about conditioning the fort for service in the upcoming war that nearly everyone assumed would soon occur.

Anderson's second-in-command was Captain Abner Doubleday, a forty-one-year-old New Yorker who had also graduated from the U.S. Military Academy and served in the Seminole and Mexican Wars, and who is probably best remembered today for his possible involvement in the "invention" of baseball.

Positioned on the mainland was Confederate General P.G.T. Beauregard, a forty-two-year-old dashingly handsome Creole from Louisiana who, it is said, learned French as a child before he spoke English. An 1838 West Point graduate who had ranked second in his class of forty-five, he began his army career in the Corps of Engineers. He was wounded twice during the Mexican War, where he was recognized for his gallantry. In the years prior to the Civil War,

Beauregard had supervised the construction of several U.S. Army coastal fortifications. He had just been appointed superintendent of West Point when he resigned his commission and accepted one in the Confederate army, whereupon he was sent to Charleston.

In early April 1861, Anderson, peering over Fort Sumter's ramparts and observing more South Carolina militia deploying on the mainland and additional artillery being placed with their barrels trained upon the fort, realized that he had little chance to defend the installation and keep it from being occupied by the local militia. The fortification was already extremely low on supplies, provisions, and weaponry, but Anderson had hoped that he might be the beneficiary of a resupply ship that he understood was nearing Charleston.

On April 8 Beauregard informed L. P. Walker, the secretary of war for the Confederate states, that he had just received information that President Abraham Lincoln was dispatching urgently needed supplies to Fort Sumter and that if force was required to deliver the materials to Major Anderson, then force would be used. Two days later Walker responded to Beauregard, ordering him to "demand the evacuation, and, if this is refused, proceed in such a manner as you may determine to reduce it." The next day, at 2:00 p.m., Beauregard sent a message to Major Anderson reminding him that the Confederacy had taken no hostile action toward him, his men, or the fort, on the assumption that he would voluntarily evacuate the structure. "But," the general added, "the Confederate States can no longer delay assuming actual possession of a fortification commanding the entrance of one of their harbors, and necessary to its defense and security." Beauregard promised Anderson that he would safely relocate him, his men, and all private and fort possessions, including personal weapons, to any post in the United States that Anderson desired.

Beauregard received the answer he did not want to hear from Anderson later the same day: "[I]t is a demand with which I regret that my sense of honor and . . . my obligations to my government prevent my compliance." Upon further orders from Walker, Beauregard, at 11:00 p.m. on the eleventh, told Anderson that the Southern army would refrain from firing upon the fort if he (Anderson) would simply decide upon a time to evacuate and not fire upon the Confederates. At 2:30 a.m. the next day, Anderson replied that he would surrender Fort Sumter by noon on April 15 if he had received no further orders from his government nor additional supplies. Fifty minutes later, Beauregard issued his final communiqué to Anderson, telling him that he would fire upon the fort "in one hour from this time."

And thus it was that during the early morning hours of April 12, 1861, Confederate batteries on the mainland commenced an awesome and deadly artillery barrage on the weathered fort. The facility's 128 defenders resisted bravely, but the intensity of the enemy cannons proved too much. On April 14, at 2:30 p.m., following two days of intense shelling by the shore batteries of the Confederates, the defeated, but still proud, Union garrison surrendered to Beauregard's command.

On April 18, from aboard the steamship *Baltic*, Anderson advised U.S. Secretary of War Simon Cameron that:

> *Having defended Fort Sumter for thirty-four hours,*
> *until the quarters were entirely burned, the main gates*
> *destroyed by fire, the gorge wall seriously injured, the*
> *magazine surrounded by flames, and its door closed*
> *from the effects of the heat, four barrels and three*
> *cartridges of powder only being available, and no*
> *provisions but pork remaining, I accepted terms of*
> *evacuation, offered by General Beauregard, being the*
> *same offered by him on the 11th instant, prior to the*

commencement of hostilities, and marched out of the
fort on Sunday afternoon, the 14th instant, with colors
flying and drums beating, bringing away company and
private property, and saluting my flag with fifty guns.

The only federal death occurred when one of the fort's cannon crew was killed by an accidental explosion during the artillery salute to the flag at the end of the incident. The falling of Fort Sumter to Confederate troops that spring day heralded the beginning of the Civil War. On April 14, 1865, the day President Lincoln was shot by John Wilkes Booth at Ford's Theatre in Washington, D.C., Anderson, now a retired brigadier general, returned to Fort Sumter to raise the very flag that he had lowered from its staff four years earlier. Anderson died, a well-respected citizen, in Charleston in October 1871.

DAMN THE TORPEDOES!

Alabama, 1864

It was early morning on August 5, 1864, and U.S. Navy Rear Admiral David Glasgow Farragut paced the floor of his small cabin aboard his flagship, the USS *Hartford,* contemplating what the next several hours might bring. The evening before, he had written to his wife, "I am going into Mobile Bay in the morning if 'God is my leader' and I hope he is."

Farragut, in charge of the navy's West Gulf Squadron, commanded fourteen wooden vessels and four ironclads, and in a few minutes, if all went well, his fleet would sail into Mobile Bay, occupy it, and deny the Confederate-held city of Mobile access to the Gulf of Mexico. He knew it would be no easy task. Not only was Mobile heavily fortified with three lines of defensive works, each containing numerous redoubts, but it was also protected by three large fortifications—Forts Morgan, Gaines, and Powell—strategically positioned at the entrance to Mobile Bay. In anticipation of the Union attack, the Confederate navy's Admiral Franklin Buchanan, who earlier in his career had been the first superintendent of the U.S. Naval Academy, patrolled the bay with three wooden ships and the powerful ironclad CSS *Tennessee.*

Farragut figured that he had two significant problems: somehow he had to safely pass Fort Morgan without having too much damage inflicted upon his fleet, and, once the ships were in the bay, he had to destroy the *Tennessee* as quickly as possible. Both were formidable objectives. Fort Morgan, built by the U.S. Army between 1818 and 1834 and named for Revolutionary War hero General Daniel Morgan, consisted of a huge, ten-sided masonry building and was fortified with sixty large artillery pieces and manned by upwards of two thousand solders. The *Tennessee* was the shining star of the Confederate navy. Measuring more than two hundred feet long, with a beam of forty-eight feet and a draft of fourteen feet, it was constructed on a yellow pine frame, covered with nearly ten inches of pine and oak wood, and enclosed with a thick outer skin of metal armor. Its weaponry consisted of six cannons.

As dawn broke, Farragut gave the command to proceed toward Mobile Bay, with one of his ships, the *Tecumseh,* leading the flotilla. It soon became evident that the Confederates had laced the entrance to the bay with an abundance of torpedoes (or, in today's nomenclature, mines), and within minutes the *Tecumseh* struck one of the explosive devices, sending it and several score of its crew to a watery grave. When Farragut, aboard the *Hartford,* was apprised of the *Tecumseh*'s ordeal and that the waters were full of torpedoes, he exclaimed, "Damn the torpedoes! Four bells! Go ahead full speed!" which, through the intervening years, has been modernized to "Damn the torpedoes! Full speed ahead!"

Farragut then steered the *Hartford* to take the lead. He had faith that his beloved ship was up to the task of defeating the Confederate naval vessels holed up in the bay. It had been built at the Boston Navy Yard in 1858, and since its launching had served as the flagship of the navy's East India Squadron. When the Civil War erupted in April 1861, it was recalled to the United States and reassigned to Farragut, who was then a captain, and his newly organized command. The vessel was 225 feet long, with a beam of 44 feet, and drew 17 feet of water. Armed with twenty-four pieces of heavy cannon, it was one of the U.S. Navy's finest ships afloat.

Despite brutal fire from the big guns at Forts Morgan and Gaines, the ships of the Union flotilla finally entered the bay, only to be confronted by Admiral Buchanan's feared ironclad, the *Tennessee*. In a fierce fight that lasted two hours, the *Tennessee* repeatedly bombarded the Union ships with blistering fire. Finally, however, Buchanan—after being attacked and fired upon by Farragut's entire fleet and having the *Tennessee*'s armor pierced and her steering apparatus disabled—surrendered the ironclad and its crew of 190. By noon the fiery Battle of Mobile Bay was over, but not before 157 Union and Confederate lives had been lost, with another 464 wounded and captured.

Ostensibly due to a wait-and-see attitude on the part of Union commanders in Washington about the outcome of Confederate General John Bell Hood's invasion of Tennessee during the fall of 1864 and the demand on Union manpower that it would bring, no effort was made by the victorious Farragut to capture the city of Mobile. The Confederate command at Fort Gaines surrendered on August 8, and Fort Morgan's garrison capitulated fifteen days later (the other Confederate installation, Fort Powell, had fallen to the Union early in the conflict).

In the aftermath of the battle, David Farragut became ill and requested leave. He was promoted to vice admiral for his victory, but saw little additional action during the last days of the war. He eventually was promoted to full admiral and served as commander of the navy's European Squadron before dying in August 1870. Franklin

Buchanan, taken prisoner after losing the *Tennessee,* was eventually paroled and hastened to Mobile just in time for the massive Union siege upon the city during late March and early April 1865. After the war, he served as president of the Maryland Agricultural College and died in May 1874.

Fort Morgan was eventually restored and is today a National Historic Landmark administered by the National Park Service. The USS *Hartford* served all around the globe before being decommissioned in 1926. The ship's final resting place was Norfolk, Virginia's U.S. Navy Yard, where, due to neglect and disinterest, she sank at her moorings in 1956. The CSS *Tennessee* was captured by Farragut, repaired, rechristened the USS *Tennessee,* and assisted the Union navy in the taking of Fort Morgan later in August 1864. The ironclad was decommissioned the following August and was scrapped in November 1867.

The Battle of Mobile Bay was arguably the Union navy's greatest victory during the Civil War. Both sides of the conflict were commanded by headstrong, professional naval officers. But, ironically, Farragut, the Union commander, was a Southerner, born on a Tennessee hardscrabble farm hundreds of miles from the ocean in the western foothills of the Appalachian Mountains. Buchanan, the Confederate leader, was a Marylander who resigned his U.S. naval commission on the assumption that his native state would elect to secede from the Union. When Maryland cast its lot with the United States instead, Buchanan tried to have his resignation rescinded but was refused, prompting him to volunteer his services to the Confederacy.

THE ASSASSINATION
OF ABRAHAM LINCOLN

District of Columbia, 1865

By the time Richard Lawrence—the man who had attempted to kill President Andrew Jackson in 1835—died alone and largely forgotten in his cramped, dirty cell at the Hospital for the Insane in Washington, D.C., the nation had elected a new president. Abraham Lincoln, like Andrew Jackson before him, was a product of the frontier, born in Kentucky and raised in Illinois. As he stepped into the presidency in early 1861, the United States was about to be torn asunder by complex states' rights issues that for the past ten years had defied peaceful resolution. Now, war between Southern and Northern factions was inevitable, and Lincoln faced a challenge that culminated in his premature death at the hands of an assassin.

The Civil War had rocked along for four long, bloody years, when in April 1865, General Robert E. Lee, leader of the Army of Northern Virginia, surrendered his command to Union General Ulysses S. Grant at Appomattox Court House, Virginia. The terrible conflict, which had taken tens of thousands of lives, had brought unimaginable devastation and pain to both the North and the South and had cost millions of dollars in property damage. But now, the carnage was at last over.

President Lincoln was still regaling in the news of the war's end when five days later he accompanied his wife, Mary, to the theater. Perhaps a few hours of light humor would provide a measure of badly needed relaxation to the president's hectic life that had been so preoccupied with the war for the past four years.

It was already dark on the evening of April 14, 1865, when President and Mrs. Lincoln arrived by carriage at Ford's Theatre, located seven blocks from the White House. Although he had been cautioned about his personal safety, the president refused police protection or the services of bodyguards. In fact, only a week or so earlier, he had dreamed that he had been assassinated, but had jokingly passed off the experience with the words, "What does anybody want to assassinate me for? . . . It is nonsense."

What was "nonsense" to Lincoln, however, was reality to John Wilkes Booth. Booth, scion of a renowned family of actors, was a Maryland-born Southerner of the old school, and his immense disappointment at Lee's surrender at Appomattox the previous week was well known to his friends and acquaintances. "My love . . . is for the South alone," he once wrote. Continuing, he added, "Nor do I deem it a dishonor in attempting to make for her a prisoner of this man [Lincoln], to whom she owes so much misery."

As early as the previous September, Booth had sought the support of two friends, Samuel Arnold and Michael O'Laughlin, in a bizarre plot to kidnap the president, surrender him to Confederate authorities, and use him as a bargaining chip in an exchange for Southern prisoners. Over the next few months, Booth confided his plans to other acquaintances, and by the spring of 1865, he had enrolled four more accomplices: John Surratt, George Atzerodt, David Herold, and Lewis Paine. By mid-March 1865, Booth's elaborate plot was ready to be executed.

Booth and his fellow conspirators met in a Washington, D.C., saloon on March 17. Over the protestations of Surratt, who had suddenly begun to question the practicality of the plan, Booth announced that they would kidnap President Lincoln three days later when he visited the nearby Soldiers' Home. Lincoln's sudden cancellation of his visit, however, sent Booth back to the drawing board.

By the time new plans could be laid, General Lee had surrendered the Confederate army, thus ending the war. The idea of simply kidnapping the president suddenly lost its importance, and Booth carefully wove a new web of intrigue. The revised plot was even more sinister than the first: This one called for the assassination of not only the president, but also of his vice president, Andrew Johnson, and of the secretary of state, William Seward. Later, when Booth learned that Lincoln and General Ulysses S. Grant would attend a play at Ford's Theatre on the night of April 14, he added Grant to his list, contacted his associates, and finalized the plans. He would personally kill the president and Grant, while Atzerodt would murder Vice President Johnson and Paine would kill Seward.

During the late afternoon of April 14, Booth and his cohorts met one final time to go over plans. Booth was furious when Atzerodt announced that he could not go through with his part of the plot. "I cannot kill Johnson," he declared. "I cannot become a murderer." At about the same time, it was learned that General Grant would not be attending the play after all, leaving only Lincoln and Seward as targets. Despite the unnerving news, Booth declared that it was too late to regroup and reconsider the scheme. Curtain call at Ford's Theatre was just minutes away, and President and Mrs. Lincoln would be arriving soon. Obviously shaken by the recent turn of events, Booth nonetheless ordered that the operation proceed.

A short time later, Booth watched as the president and his wife entered Ford's Theatre. He then proceeded down the street to a saloon, where he spent the next couple hours drinking. At around 10:00 p.m., he left the saloon, walked back to Ford's, entered the theater with what an observer called "a wild look in his eyes," and climbed the stairs to President Lincoln's reserved box. With the Lincolns were two young acquaintances, Major Henry Reed Rathbone and his fiancée, Clara Harris.

The play, *Our American Cousin,* was in the third act when Booth entered the box from the rear, fired his single-shot Derringer at the back of the president's head, and in the ensuing scuffle, slashed Major Rathbone's arm with a knife. With all eyes in the theater upon him, Booth screamed *"Sic semper tyrannis!"* (Ever thus to tyrants) and leaped from the box onto the stage below. A flag draping one of the boxes caught a spur on one of the assassin's boots, causing him to injure his leg when he hit the stage. Quickly making his way out the building's back door, he mounted his awaiting horse and galloped away in pain.

President Lincoln was carried to a house across the street, where he died the following morning just after seven o'clock. In the meantime, Lewis Paine had boggled his attempt on Secretary Seward's life and was arrested soon afterward, along with Mary Surratt, John's mother, who appears to have been guilty of nothing more than temporarily housing Paine in her boardinghouse. The other conspirators fled in various directions.

Booth stopped at Dr. Samuel Mudd's house in Maryland for a quick check on his injured leg, then rode south into Virginia. Near the village of Port Royal Cross Roads, he and fellow conspirator David Herold holed up in a barn owned by Richard Garrett. On April 26 U.S. Army troops located the two fugitives in the barn and demanded their surrender. Herold, frightened out of his wits, gave himself up, but when the reluctant Booth made a run for it after the troops had set the barn ablaze, he was shot and killed.

During the middle of the following July, Atzerodt, Paine, Herold, and Mrs. Surratt were all hanged from the gallows at the Old Penitentiary in Washington. O'Laughlin was sentenced to life imprisonment, as was Dr. Mudd, whom President Andrew Johnson later pardoned. Samuel Arnold also received a prison term. John Surratt made good his escape, but was eventually located in Egypt and returned to the United States for trial. His case was tossed out of court, and he lived the rest of his life in Baltimore.

BIBLIOGRAPHY

Abernethy, Thomas Perkins. *The Burr Conspiracy.* New York: Oxford University Press, 1954.

Adams, George Rollie. *General William S. Harney: Prince of Dragoons.* Lincoln: University of Nebraska Press, 2001.

Alvord, Clarence Walworth, and Lee Bidgood. *The First Explorations of the Trans-Allegheny Region by the Virginians 1650–1674.* Cleveland, OH: Arthur H. Clark Company, 1912. Reprint, Baltimore, MD: Clearfield Company, 1996.

American State Papers, Indian Affairs. Vol. 2. Washington, DC: Gales and Seaton, 1832.

Andrist, Ralph K., ed. *George Washington: A Biography in His Own Words.* New York: Newsweek, 1972.

Baily, Francis. *Journal of a Tour in Unsettled Parts of North America in 1796 & 1797.* Carbondale: Southern Illinois University Press, 1969.

Barbour Philip L., ed. *The Jamestown Voyages Under the First Charter 1606–1609.* 2 vols. London: Cambridge University Press, 1969.

Clarke, James W. *American Assassins: The Darker Side of Politics.* Princeton, NJ: Princeton University Press, 1982.

Crockett, David. *A Narrative of the Life of David Crockett and the State of Tennessee.* Philadelphia: E. L. Carey and A. Hart, 1834. Reprint, Lincoln: University of Nebraska Press, 1987.

Crutchfield, James A. *The Natchez Trace: A Pictorial History.* Nashville, TN: Rutledge Hill Press, 1985. Reprint, 2007.

———. *Tennesseans at War.* Nashville, TN: Rutledge Hill Press, 1987.

Cumming, William P., ed. *The Discoveries of John Lederer with Unpublished Letters by and about Lederer to Governor John Winthrop, Jr.* Charlottesville: University of Virginia Press, 1958.

Davis, Edwin Adams, and William Ransom Hogan. *William Johnson's Natchez: The Ante-Bellum Diary of a Free Negro.* Baton Rouge: Louisiana State University Press, 1951.

———. *The Barber of Natchez.* Baton Rouge, LA: Louisiana State University, 1954.

Dillon, Richard H. *North American Indian Wars.* New York: Facts on File, 1983.

Drimmer, Frederick, ed. *Captured by the Indians: 15 Firsthand Accounts, 1750–1870.* New York: Dover Publications, 1985.

Eckert, Allan W. *The Court-Martial of Daniel Boone.* Ashland, KY: Jesse Stuart Foundation, 2005. (Author's note: Although this book is a fictional account of the subject, it is accurate, engaging, and worthy of citation here.)

Faragher, John Mack. *Daniel Boone: The Life and Legend of an American Pioneer.* New York: Holt Paperbacks, 1993.

Faust, Patricia L., ed. *Historical Times Illustrated Encyclopedia of the Civil War.* New York: Harper & Row, 1986.

Fisher, Vardis. *Suicide or Murder? The Strange Death of Governor Meriwether Lewis.* Chicago: Swallow Press, 1962.

Flexner, James Thomas. *Washington: The Indispensable Man.* Boston: Little, Brown, 1974.

Grant, Bruce. *American Forts Yesterday and Today.* New York: E. P. Dutton, 1965.

Harper's Pictorial History of the Civil War. New York: Fairfax Press, 1977.

Hays, Wilma Pitchford. *Eli Whitney: Founder of Modern Industry.* New York: Franklin Watts, 1965.

Hodge, Frederick Webb, ed. *Handbook of American Indians North of Mexico.* Washington, DC: Smithsonian Institution, Bureau of American Ethnology, 1910.

Jackson, Donald, ed. *Letters of the Lewis and Clark Expedition with Related Documents 1783–1854.* 2 vols. Urbana: University of Illinois Press, 1978.

Jahoda, Gloria. *The Trail of Tears.* New York: Wings Books, 1995.

Johnson, Charles. *A General History of the Robberies & Murders of the Most Notorious Pirates.* Guilford, CT: Lyons Press, n.d.

Lee, Robert E. *Blackbeard the Pirate: A Reappraisal of His Life and Times.* Winston-Salem, NC: John F. Blair, 1974.

Lewis, Emanuel Raymond. *Seacoast Fortifications of the United States: An Introductory History.* Annapolis, MD: Leeward Publications, 1979.

Little, Thomas Vance. "The Tennessee Years of Thomas Hart Benton," in *The Tennessee Valley Historical Review* 2, no. 3. Nashville, TN: Blue and Gray Press, 1973.

Long, E. B. *The Civil War Day by Day: An Almanac 1861–1865.* With Barbara Long. Garden City, NY: Doubleday, 1971.

Lorant, Stefan, ed. *The New World: The First Pictures of America.* New York: Duell, Sloan and Pearce, 1965.

Merrill, Boynton, Jr. *Jefferson's Nephews.* Princeton, NJ: Princeton University Press, 1976.

Morris, Celia. *Fanny Wright: Rebel in America.* Chicago: University of Illinois Press, 1992.

North Carolina History Project, http://northcarolinahistory.org/encyclopedia.

Parks, Edd Winfield. "Dreamer's Vision: Frances Wright at Nashoba (1825–1830)," in *Tennessee Historial Magazine,* Series II, Volume II, no. 2. Nashville: TN Historical Society, 1932.

Peake, Ora Brooks. *A History of the United States Indian Factory System: 1795–1822.* Denver, CO: Sage Books, 1954.

Plaisance, Aloysius Frederick. "The United States Government Factory System: 1796–1822." Dissertation, Saint Louis University. Privately published, 1954.

Remini, Robert V. *The Battle of New Orleans.* New York: Penguin Books, 1999.

———. *Andrew Jackson and His Indian Wars.* New York: Penguin Books, 2001.

Robertson, David. *Denmark Vesey: The Buried History of America's Largest Slave Rebellion and the Man Who Led It.* New York: Alfred A. Knopf, 1999.

Rothert, Otto A. *The Outlaws of Cave-In-Rock: Historical Accounts of the Famous Highwaymen and River Pirates Who Operated in Pioneer Days upon the Ohio and Mississippi Rivers and over the Old Natchez Trace.* Cleveland, OH: Arthur H. Clark Company, 1924.

Silver, James W. *Edmund Pendleton Gaines: Frontier General.* Baton Rouge: Louisiana State University Press, 1949.

Steele, William O. *The Wilderness Tattoo: A Narrative of Juan Ortiz.* New York: Harcourt Brace Jovanovich, 1972.

Utley, Robert M., and Wilcomb E. Washburn. *The American Heritage History of the Indian Wars.* New York: American Heritage Publishing Company, 1977.

Wellman, Paul I. *Spawn of Evil: The Invisible Empire of Soulless Men Which for a Generation Held the Nation in a Spell of Terror.* Garden City, NY: Doubleday, 1964.

Williams, Samuel Cole, ed. *Adair's History of the American Indians.* Nashville, TN: Blue and Gray Press, 1971.

INDEX

ABOUT THE AUTHOR

James A. Crutchfield is a western historian who has written numerous books, including *It Happened in Texas, It Happened in Washington,* and seven other It Happened In titles; forty books about American history; and hundreds of articles for newspapers, journals, and national magazines, among them *The Magazine Antiques, Early American Life,* and *The American Cowboy.* He has won writing awards from Western Writers of America, the American Association for State and Local History, and the Tennessee Revolutionary Bicentennial Commission. A former board member of the Tennessee Historical Society, he sits on the Board of National Scholars for President's Park in Williamsburg, Virginia. He and his wife, Regena, reside in a pre–Civil War home in Tennessee.